Happy Endings

Finishing the Edges of Your Quilt

REVISED EDITION

MIMI DIETRICH

CREDITS

President ♥ Nancy J. Martin
CEO ♥ Daniel J. Martin
Publisher ♥ Jane Hamada
Editorial Director ♥ Mary V. Green
Managing Editor ♥ Tina Cook
Technical Editor ♥ Karen Costello Soltys
Copy Editor ♥ Liz McGehee
Design Director ♥ Stan Green
Illustrator ♥ Laurel Strand
Cover and Text Designer ♥ Regina Girard
Photographer ♥ Brent Kane
Indexer ♥ Kim C. Smith

That Patchwork Place® is an imprint
of Martingale & Company®.

Happy Endings: Finishing the Edges of Your Quilt,
Revised Edition
© 1987, 2003 by Mimi Dietrich

First edition 1987
Revised edition 2003

Martingale & Company
20205 144th Avenue NE
Woodinville, WA 98072-8478 USA
www.martingale-pub.com

Printed in China
08 07 06 05 04 03   8 7 6 5 4 3 2 1

Library of Congress Cataloging-in-Publication Data

Dietrich, Mimi.
  Happy endings / Mimi Dietrich.
    p. cm.
  ISBN 1-56477-500-3
  1. Quilting. 2. Patchwork. 3. Borders, Ornamental
(Decorative arts) I. Title.
  TT835 .D53 2003
  746.46'041—dc21

                                          2003008962

MISSION STATEMENT
*Dedicated to providing quality products
and service to inspire creativity.*

Dedication
For my family

She remembered the phone call. She had just finished the quilt. I called then, she told me she was done, but there was an edge to her voice. She felt funny about it, couldn't explain the feeling.

"You feel sad," I said.

She remembered that. How did I know?

The fun in creating it, the joy in doing it, that was gone with the quilt finished. It was true. She did feel sad.

A friend once called her a process person. Quilters and writers use the same language. We both like holding the finished product in our hands, but the important thing is the process. We want to stay in it as long as we can and do it as well as we can.

Ending a quilt is a process. There's a joy in the doing. So if it must end, let it be a happy ending.

A Writer's Journal
—John Haw
April 1987

Contents

*M*ore than 15 years ago, I received a phone call from a quilting teacher in the Baltimore area, proposing an idea for a book. That teacher was Mimi Dietrich, and her *Happy Endings* book, first published in 1987, has been one of our all-time bestselling titles.

Why is this so? All quiltmakers need to employ these basic steps to finish their quilts. A quilt that has been made with loving and painstaking stitches needs to have an equally special edge finish. And Mimi's book has provided the perfect resource guide for choosing the appropriate binding or finishing technique.

Easy-to-follow, step-by-step directions by this master teacher make this an ideal book for beginners. But even seasoned quilters need to be reminded of the myriad options available for a special quilt finish.

From traditional double-fold binding to more unusual edge treatments, such as piping or rickrack, Mimi will inspire you to try any number of edge treatments. And she doesn't stop there. Helpful hints for mitering border corners, layering and basting your quilt, adding hanging sleeves, making a finishing-touch label, and more are all part of the new and improved *Happy Endings*. And this time around, all the samples and illustrations are shown in full color.

Over the years, Mimi and I have shared many *Happy Endings* anecdotes, stories, and jokes. They have ranged from a funeral home named Happy Endings to titles of risqué romance novels. But my favorite happy ending is that after 15 years, quiltmakers still appreciate a basic book that functions as a complete guide to quilt finishing.

Nancy J. Martin

President of Martingale & Company
Woodinville, Washington, 2003

Choosing a Happy Ending for Your Quilt

Happy Endings has taken me on a wonderful journey through the world of quilting. I have written other books, taught classes to delightful groups in fabulous places, and met quilters from all over the world. As it turned out, *Happy Endings* was really only a beginning!

In this new, improved edition of *Happy Endings,* I added border techniques to help you achieve flat, straight edges on your quilts. If you sew borders on your quilt properly, the edges of your quilt will not ripple and your binding will be neat. This book now contains all the information you'll need to finish the edges of your quilt with borders and binding.

As you browse through the pages, you'll find "Happy Ending Hints" to guide you to success. And some techniques are labeled with "Mimi's Favorite," to indicate the techniques I use most often in finishing my quilts. So please don't tuck this book away on the shelf! Put it in a special place in your sewing area, right next to your sewing machine, so that you'll have the information at hand each time you're ready to stitch borders or bindings on a new quilt.

Quilters love to choose fabric colors, textures, and prints to create new designs for our quilts. We find a wonderful peace in quilting the layers of soft fabric. But many of us hastily complete the last steps of the quiltmaking process—finishing the edges. Many books, magazines, and patterns simply say, "Bind the quilt edges." *Happy Endings* gives you choices and easy-to-follow, step-by-step directions so that this stage of making your quilt can also be creative.

As you plan your quilt, consider the technique that will frame your design. There are many methods for finishing the edges of your quilted project, for encasing the batting and cut edges of the front and back of the quilt. The style of your quilt may determine the appearance of your final border. The quilt's purpose may determine the durability of your finishing method. Your time and available fabric may also be a factor as you complete your quilt. If you are planning to enter your quilt in a show, you will be looking for the perfect happy ending. This book will help you make an appropriate choice for the finishing touch on your special quilt. Whether you choose a quick front-to-back finish, use the back of the quilt to create self-binding, make your own binding, or add special effects, may all of your quilts have "happy endings"!

Mimi Dietrich

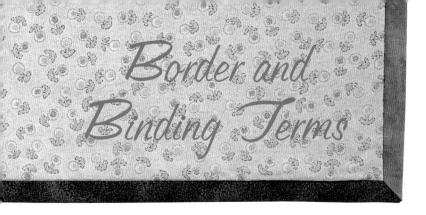

Border and Binding Terms

A quick reference to commonly used quilt-making terms.

Fabric Grain

Straight grain: The straight threads that run the length (lengthwise grain) or width (crosswise grain) of the fabric. The lengthwise grain has no stretch, and the crosswise grain has a little stretch.

Bias: True bias is measured at a 45° angle to the lengthwise and crosswise threads in the fabric. Fabric has the greatest stretch when cut on the true bias.

Borders

Borders: Strips of fabric framing the interior portion of a quilt. Borders can be whole strips of fabric, pieced patchwork, or appliquéd strips.

Overlapped corners: When borders are applied to opposite edges of your quilt, usually to the sides first, then to the top and bottom, they will overlap in the corners.

Mitered corners: Borders that are stitched together in the corners with a diagonal seam extending from the corner of the quilt design to the outer corner of the finished quilt.

Multiple-fabric borders: Borders made using two or more fabrics.

Binding

Binding: Fabric strips stitched to the edges of a quilt and folded over to encase the raw edges of the quilt top, batting, and backing.

Single-fold binding: A single layer of fabric folded over the edge of the quilt. Also called *traditional binding.*

Double-fold binding: Fabric folded in half to make a double layer of binding on your quilt. Also called *French binding.*

Stitches

Blind stitch: A nearly invisible, small hand stitch used to attach the folded edge of the binding to the back of the quilt and finish the mitered corners. Also called *appliqué stitch.*

Slip stitch: A nearly invisible, small hand stitch that works well on any straight area, such as binding or quilt sleeves. Also called *ladder stitch.*

Tools and Supplies

You need basic quilting supplies to finish your quilt. You probably have most of these supplies in your sewing room.

Sewing machine: Make sure your sewing machine is in good working order. If you haven't used it in a long time, treat it to a professional cleaning and oiling. Make sure you have a sharp needle with no bumps or burrs on it.

Walking foot or even-feed foot: This sewing-machine attachment helps feed the quilt layers under the needle at the same pace. It works in tandem with the feed dogs. The walking foot is particularly helpful for basting the edges of your quilt and applying binding.

Thread: Use all-purpose sewing thread to attach the borders and binding to your quilt.

Needles: Short needles (called *Betweens*) are used for hand quilting. Longer needles (Sharps or milliners) are used for hand stitching and finishing touches.

Pins: Use long straight pins to pin the borders to your quilt. Use safety pins to baste your quilt before machine quilting.

Tape measure: Use a metal or plastic tape measure to accurately measure your quilt.

Masking tape: Use 1"-wide masking tape to hold mitered-border corners in place while you sew them.

Scissors: Use a good, sharp pair of comfortable shears to cut fabric accurately. A small pair of embroidery scissors comes in handy for hand sewing.

Rotary cutter: This cutting tool has a round razorlike blade. Use it with a ruler and mat to cut fabric straight. The blade is extremely sharp and should be used with great care.

Rotary-cutting rulers: There are a variety of heavy acrylic rulers in different sizes that you can use with the rotary cutter. Use a 6" x 12" or 6" x 24" ruler to cut strips for borders and bindings. Use a square ruler to square up mitered borders.

Cutting mat: You need a surface made for cutting fabric with the rotary cutter. This mat protects your table and helps keep the rotary blade sharp.

Iron: Use a good steam iron to press seams and to press the fold in the binding.

Low-loft batting: A thin batting makes it easier to control the quilt layers as you sew the binding on your quilt.

Binding clips: Use these clips (which are actually hair clips) to hold your quilt binding firmly in place while you hand stitch the back.

Basic Border Techniques

When you have completed the quilt blocks and stitched the quilt top together, borders add a finishing frame to your quilt. They complement your quilt, much like the matting and frame on a painting.

Measuring Your Quilt for Borders

Even if you're making a quilt from a pattern or project book that gives border measurements, it's important to measure your completed quilt top before you cut your borders. If you're making a large quilt or a quilt with many patchwork pieces, the sides of your quilt top may vary in size from the stated measurements because everyone pieces a little differently. For this reason, it's always a good idea to cut the borders to match the actual measurements of your quilt top.

Mimi's Favorite

This is it—the most important border tip in the book! Always measure the quilt through its center to determine the cut length of the border strips. A center measurement is more accurate because the edges of the quilt may stretch. Measuring through the center also helps avoid rippled borders in the finished quilt. Careful measuring techniques will result in smooth, even borders on your quilt!

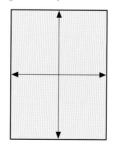

Cutting Border Strips

Always cut borders on the straight grain of the fabric, never on the bias. Bias edges stretch out of shape easily. Cut your borders using a rotary cutter and a long ruler or use a pair of sharp scissors. To make the best use of your yardage, follow these tips for cutting borders:

- If your border length is 20" or less, cut two borders at a time across the folded fabric width.

- If your border length is between 20" and 40", cut one border at a time across the width of a single layer of fabric.

- If your border length is more than 40", cut two borders at a time along the length of a double layer of fabric.

- If you do not have enough fabric to cut a full-length border strip, you can piece the border.

- When you cut borders with a rotary cutter and a ruler, it is important to cut perfectly straight across your folded fabric; otherwise, when you open the strip, you'll notice it's V shaped.

Happy Ending Hint

When making larger quilts, you may find it difficult to cut long borders. So why not tear it instead? To "cut" long borders, just make a small clip at the edge of the fabric and tear along the straight grain. You can tear borders on the lengthwise grain, but be careful on the crosswise grain—the edges may stretch.

Adding Borders with Overlapped Corners

These are the easiest borders to apply to your quilt. Two side borders are stitched to the quilt first, and then the top and bottom borders are added. No mitering or fussing is needed!

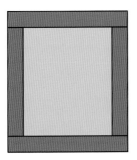

Overlapped Corners

1. Measure the length of the quilt top, from top to bottom, through the center. Cut two side border strips to this measurement. Fold each side border in half to find the center and mark with a straight pin or by pinching a crease at the fold. Fold each quilt edge in half and also mark the centers.

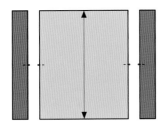

Measure center of quilt,
top to bottom. Mark centers.

2. With right sides together and raw edges aligned, pin the side borders to the quilt top, matching the center pins and the ends. If necessary, ease each half of the quilt to fit the borders. Sew the border to the quilt using a ¼" seam allowance. Press the seam allowances toward the borders.

3. Measure the width of the quilt top, from side to side, through the center, including the borders you just attached. Cut the top and bottom border strips to this measurement. Mark the center points of the border strips and quilt top, and pin the borders to the quilt top as you did for the side borders. Stitch the borders to the quilt and press as before.

Measure center of quilt,
side to side. Mark centers.

3. Fold the borders in half to find the center and mark each with a pin. Also mark half the quilt-top measurement with a pin near each end of each border strip. In our example, if the quilt top is 60" long, measure 30" from the center marking and put a pin at this measurement. Repeat for the other end of the border.

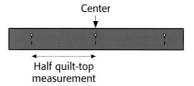

Center

Half quilt-top measurement

Adding Borders with Mitered Corners

Mitered borders have a diagonal seam where two border strips meet in the corners, extending from the corner of the pieced or appliquéd section of the quilt to the outer corner. This corner treatment is a little more formal than overlapped corners.

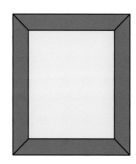

Mitered Corners

1. Before adding the mitered border, use a rotary-cutting ruler to make sure that each corner of your quilt is perfectly square. Trim if necessary.

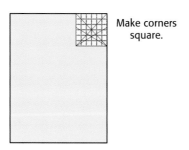

Make corners square.

2. Measure the quilt top from raw edge to raw edge, including the seam allowances. For first the length, then the width of your quilt top, add two times the cut width of your borders, plus 4". For instance, if your quilt top measures 60" long and you're planning to add 6" borders, add 60" + 6" + 6" + 4" = 76". Cut two side borders to this length. Repeat the calculations for the top and bottom borders, adding 6" + 6" + 4", or 16" to the width of your quilt top.

4. With right sides together and center pins matching, pin one border strip to the quilt top. Also match the outer pins to the raw edges of the quilt top. Stitch, leaving ¼" of the quilt top unstitched at the beginning and end of each seam; backstitch. Press the seams toward the borders. Repeat for all four borders.

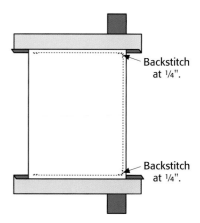

Backstitch at ¼".

Backstitch at ¼".

5. With the right side up, place the first corner to be mitered on your ironing board. Pin the quilt to the ironing board to keep it from pulling and the corner from slipping. Position the quilt and borders as shown, with the vertical border overlapping the horizontal border.

Quilt top

6. Fold the vertical border under at a 45° angle. Adjust the fold so that the borders meet evenly as shown. Place pins through all layers at the fold. Place your rotary-cutting ruler over the corner to check that the corner is flat and square. Adjust the border for a perfect miter if necessary. When everything is straight and square, remove the pins and press the fold with a steam iron.

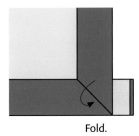

Fold.

7. Carefully center a piece of 1"-wide masking tape over the mitered fold. It will hold the miter in place as you sew.

8. Unpin the quilt from the ironing board and turn down the vertical border, folding the center section of the quilt diagonally. Lightly draw a pencil line in the pressed crease. Carefully align the long edges of the border strips.

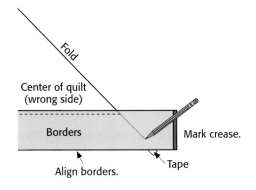

Fold

Center of quilt (wrong side)

Borders

Align borders.

Mark crease.

Tape

9. Sew on the pencil line, through the two borders, being careful not to sew through the tape. Remove the tape. You've made your first miter!

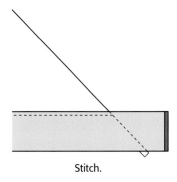

Stitch.

10. From the right side of the quilt, check to make sure that the borders lie flat; then trim the excess fabric, leaving a ¼"-wide seam allowance. Press the seam open for a perfectly mitered corner.

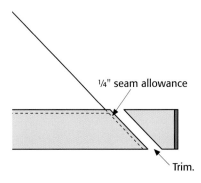

¼" seam allowance

Trim.

11. Repeat steps 5–10 for the remaining three mitered corners.

Happy Ending Hint

If you wish, you can use hand appliqué stitches to complete the mitered corner. Instead of using masking tape, pin the miter carefully. Appliqué the fold; then trim the excess fabric. Press the seam to one side.

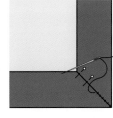

Appliqué the fold.

Overlapped corners

Mitered corners

Adding Multiple Borders

Quite often, quilts have more than one border, from a simple inner and outer border to more complex combinations. Multiple borders often graduate in size, becoming wider toward the outer edge of the quilt. You can overlap or miter the corners (or substitute corner squares), depending on the look you desire.

Overlapped Corners

1. Measure the quilt top and cut the inner border strips, following the directions for "Adding Borders with Overlapped Corners" on page 13. Measure and cut the outer borders after you have applied the first border.
2. Sew each border to the quilt one round at a time, sewing all four strips of the same fabric before adding strips of the next fabric. Press the seam allowances toward the outer edge of the quilt.

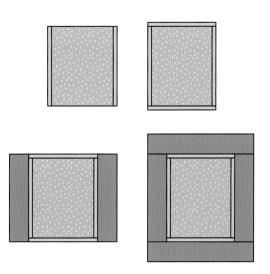

Mitered Corners

If you're planning to add two or more borders to your quilt, you can sew individual strips of each fabric together to create the multiple border for each side of the quilt, and then attach the borders and miter each corner as a unit.

1. Measure the quilt top and cut the border strips, following the directions for "Adding Borders with Mitered Corners" on page 14. Be sure to take into consideration the width of each border you'll be adding, not just one.
2. Sew the border strips together to make four complete borders, one for each side of the quilt.

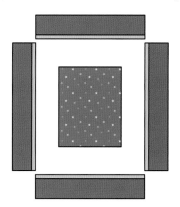

3. Treat these multiple-fabric borders as single borders and carefully sew them to the quilt top, following the directions for "Adding Borders with Mitered Corners." As you fold, pin, and tape the miters, be sure to carefully align the individual border seams for perfectly matched corners.

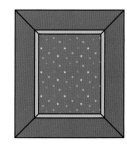

To ensure that the method you choose to finish your quilt works just as nicely as you planned, I'd like to share a few techniques for the quilting process to make sure your quilted project lies nice and square and that the raw edges are ready for whatever binding method you choose.

Selecting the Quilt Backing

Choose a fabric for the back of your quilt that complements the quilt top. Repeat a fabric from the quilt design or find a print with the colors of the quilt. A solid fabric will show off the quilting design, while a print fabric will hide any flaws in your quilting. Do not use a bed sheet for the back of your quilt if you will be hand quilting. You will have problems stitching through the high thread count fabric.

Mimi's Favorite

I like to use print fabrics for the back of my quilts to complement the quilt design. When I hand quilt, I don't worry what the quilting looks like on the back. The print fabric also "invites" me to pick up the quilt and stitch.

Piecing the Backing

The backing should be larger than the quilt top. For a small wall quilt or baby quilt, the backing should be at least 2" larger on all sides. For a large quilt, the backing should be 4" to 6" larger on all sides. If your quilt is wider than 40", you'll need to piece the backing. The seam can be vertical or horizontal.

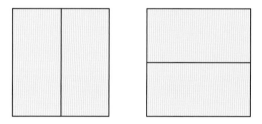

If you need two strips for your quilt backing, avoid placing a seam in the center of your quilt. A center seam will receive wear each time you fold the quilt, and it will eventually weaken.

1. After cutting your backing fabric into two sections, cut one of them in half vertically.

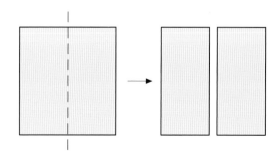

2. Sew the two narrower pieces to either side of the full-width backing piece.

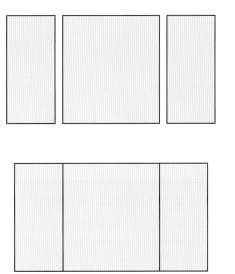

3. Press the seams open to distribute the thickness of the seams.

Happy Ending Hint

Some quilters like to use fabric scraps from the quilt top to piece a creative backing for a quilt. This is a great use of leftover fabric and adds interest to the back of the quilt.

Choosing Batting

Quilt shops carry a variety of battings. They come in different fibers: cotton, polyester, wool, blends, and even silk. And you can choose from different thicknesses that will give your quilt a puffy loft or a thinner, old-fashioned charm.

As you make small quilts, try different battings for your projects. You will soon find a batting that appeals to you. You might like the way it looks when it's finished, how it feels as you hand quilt, how it works with your machine, or the way it handles when you apply the binding. I use light-colored background fabrics for appliquéd quilts, so I always use bleached cotton batting. Natural or unbleached batting may contain darker cotton pieces that can show through light fabrics.

Make sure you read the product information on the batting labels regarding the amount of quilting required and instructions for laundering. You will soon find your personal preference.

Mimi's Favorite

I like the old-fashioned look of a thin cotton batting. I also like the way it feels when I hand quilt, and it makes it easy to control the quilt layers when I apply the binding. If you want even more of an antique look to your quilt, wash it when it's complete and the cotton batting will shrink a little, giving your quilt a slightly crinkled effect.

Cutting Batting to Size

As with quilt backing, cut your batting larger than the quilt top. Otherwise, as you quilt, the batting could slip under the quilt top and end up being too small. You can always trim it to size later.

For a small wall quilt or baby quilt, the batting should be at least 1" to 2" larger on all sides of the quilt. For a large quilt, the batting should be 4" to 6" larger on all sides.

If necessary, stitch together two pieces of batting to make one large enough to fit your quilt. Lay the pieces on a flat surface so that their edges overlap slightly. With scissors, cut through the overlapped section and remove the two narrow trimmings. Now the batting edges are butted exactly together. Simply whipstitch them together by hand with light-colored thread. Don't pull too tightly or the butted edges will pucker.

Layering and Basting a Quilt

1. Press the quilt backing so that it is smooth. Make sure that the backing is larger than the quilt top all the way around.
2. If the batting is wrinkled from being in a package, let it relax overnight or fluff it in your clothes dryer for about 15 minutes on the lowest setting before using it.
3. Press the quilt top so that all the seams are flat.
4. Place the backing on a smooth surface, right side down. Use masking tape to fasten the corners and sides of the fabric to the surface.
5. Place the batting on the backing, smoothing out any wrinkles but taking care not to stretch it out of shape.
6. Lay the quilt top, right side up, on top of the batting. Pin the three layers together in several places.
7. If you plan to hand quilt, use a long needle and light-colored thread for basting. Start in the center and baste a large X in the center of the quilt. Then baste lines parallel to the quilt edges in both directions to hold the layers together. Space the basting lines 4" to 6" apart. The more rows of basting you use, the better your layers will stay together. Baste around the outside edges about ⅛" from the edge.

If you plan to machine quilt, use safety pins to baste the layers together at 4" to 6" intervals. You can take a pin out of the quilt as you approach it with your machine, whereas stitching over thread basting can prove frustrating when it's time to pull out the basting threads.

Quilting Tips for a Happy Ending

When it comes to quilting your project, you can choose hand quilting or machine quilting, or you can hire a professional long-arm machine quilter to do the quilting for you. For detailed instructions on hand quilting, consult *Loving Stitches,* revised edition, by Jeana Kimball (Martingale & Company, 2003). For machine quilting, refer to *Machine Quilting Made Easy* by Maurine Noble (That Patchwork Place, 1994).

To achieve a happy ending with your quilt, it is important to quilt your project with an even amount of quilting. Whether it's hand or machine quilted, you can end up with puckered edges if some areas of the quilt are heavily quilted (such as with tiny stippling) while other areas are sparsely quilted. That's not to say that you have to do the same type of quilting across the entire surface of the quilt. Just try to balance the amount of quilting from area to area.

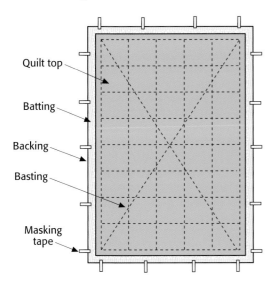

Quilt top

Batting

Backing

Basting

Masking tape

Finishing Edges without Binding

*S*ome quilts are finished without binding. Simply sew the front and back of the quilt together by hand or machine to encase the batting and all raw edges of the fabric. Use this fast-and-easy technique when you do not want a row of binding on the edge of your quilt or when you do not have binding fabric to match your quilt.

This method is often used to finish comforters or quilts that will be tied or scantily quilted. A row of hand or machine quilting near the edge can give the illusion of binding. This edge treatment is called an "envelope edge."

Finishing by Hand

If the quilting is already completed on your quilt, sew the front and back of the quilt together by hand. It is important, however, that no quilting stitches are within ½" of the quilt edges to allow space to turn under the edges.

1. Trim the back of the quilt so that the cut edges of both the quilt top and backing are ¼" larger than the finished size of the quilt. Carefully trim the batting ⅛" smaller than the finished size of the quilt. Fold the front of the quilt over the batting, turning under the ¼" seam.

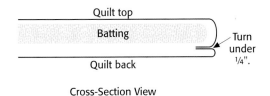

Cross-Section View

2. Turn the back of the quilt under ¼" and pin the folded edge to match the front of the quilt.

3. Stitch the front and back folded edges together using a slip stitch.

Finishing by Machine

If you want to finish your unbound quilt by machine, you'll need to sew the edges together before you quilt your project. This method works best when you are planning to tie the quilt or quilt it sparingly. It is difficult to quilt a large area closely after the edges have been stitched because the layers can shift. This is a good method to use for a child's fluffy quilt or a comforter.

1. Place the quilt top and backing right sides together. Pin the edges. If necessary, trim the back even with the front.

2. Sew a ¼"-wide seam around the four sides of the quilt, leaving an opening on one side. The opening should not be near the corner. Backstitch at the starting and stopping points to secure the stitching so that it won't come undone when you turn the quilt right side out.

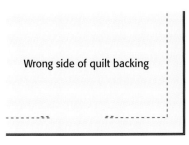

Quilt Top and Backing,
Right Sides Together

Happy Ending Hint

For a small quilt, the opening should be 6" to 10"; for a large quilt, the opening may need to be as large as 20".

3. Smooth out the batting on a flat surface and lay the inside-out quilt on top of it. Make sure the quilt top, not the backing fabric, is facing the batting. Pin the quilt to the batting. Pin around all edges of the quilt and batting, letting the batting extend beyond the quilt. The batting will be trimmed later.

   Using a basting stitch, sew the quilt to the batting, batting side down. Follow the ¼" seam allowance on the back and leave the same opening as before. Because of the thickness, it's a good idea to use your walking foot or even-feed foot for this step.

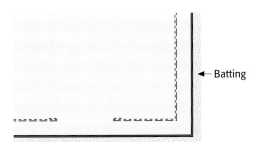

4. Trim the batting close to the stitching, making sure you do not cut the quilt top or backing fabric. Then to turn the quilt right side out, reach through the opening between the front and back of the quilt. Pull the corners through the opening, one at a time, to turn the quilt right side out. As you turn each corner, fold the two seam allowances over the batting before you pull it out, which will create pointed corners when it is turned right side out.

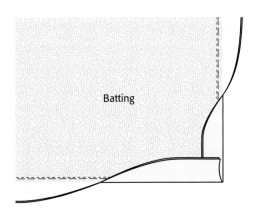

5. At the opening, fold the front seam allowance over the batting. Turn the quilt backing under ¼" and pin it to the quilt top. Stitch the opening together using the slip stitch. Or, if you prefer to do the entire process by machine, you can stitch very close to the edge using the straight stitch on your machine.

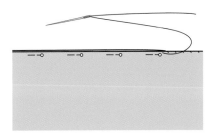

6. Before quilting or tying your project, it's important to straighten it out. A small quilt can be straightened on a tabletop, but a large quilt may require a large floor area and the help of a friend. Tug on opposite sides of the quilt to straighten the three layers of the quilt so that the front, back, and batting lie smoothly. Baste or pin the three layers together before quilting or tying.

Finishing Rounded Corners

Before sewing the front and back together, you can soften the look of the corners on your quilt or comforter by rounding off the square corners. Rounding off the corners works well if your quilt has wide borders or wide areas of background fabric in the corners of the design. However, if the quilt has a definite square pattern in the corners, it will look better if you keep the corners square.

1. Mark the rounded corners using a round dish. Use a cup for a slightly rounded corner, a saucer for a midsize rounded curve, or a dinner plate for a large rounded corner. Position the plate in one corner on the wrong side of the quilt top. The circle should touch adjacent sides of the quilt.

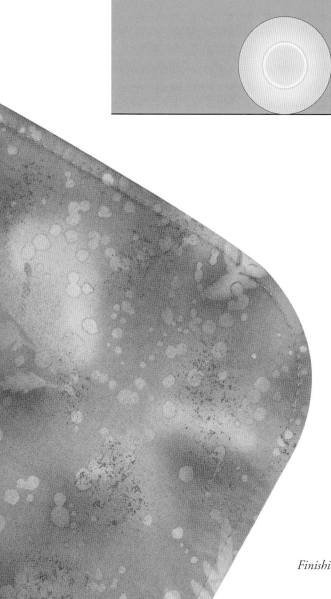

2. Use a pencil to draw along the curve from side to side, creating a perfectly rounded corner. Repeat on all four corners of the quilt top.

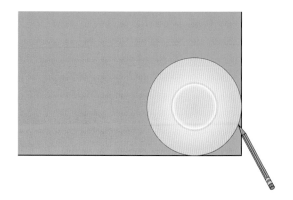

3. Using a ¼" seam allowance, sew the front and back of the quilt together as in "Finishing by Machine" on page 20, being careful not to stretch your fabric as you sew around the curves.

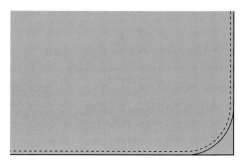

4. Trim the rounded corners of your quilt ¼" outside the seam.

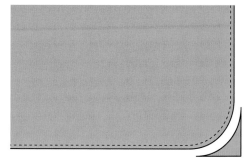

5. Attach batting, trim, and turn right side out.

Making an Imitation Binding

After you have stitched the front and the back of the quilt together and have turned it right side out, you can create the look of binding along the edge.

Sew a row of hand or machine quilting ¼" to ½" from the edge of the quilt to give the illusion of binding. The stitching also flattens the puffy edge. This effect looks especially nice when the backing fabric is the same as the border fabric on the front—it completes the illusion of an actual applied binding.

To give the appearance of wide binding, stitch a 1"- to 2"-wide border on your quilt before you finish the edges. Sew the front and the back of the quilt together by hand or machine, and then quilt in the ditch along the border seam. This last border will appear to be wide binding.

Appliquéing the Edges to a Border

To create a very unusual finishing touch, you can appliqué the edges of a curved or scalloped quilt (such as a Wedding Ring quilt or one that simply has a scalloped border) to a straight border. Your quilt will still have that nice scalloped look, but you won't have to bind the curved edges.

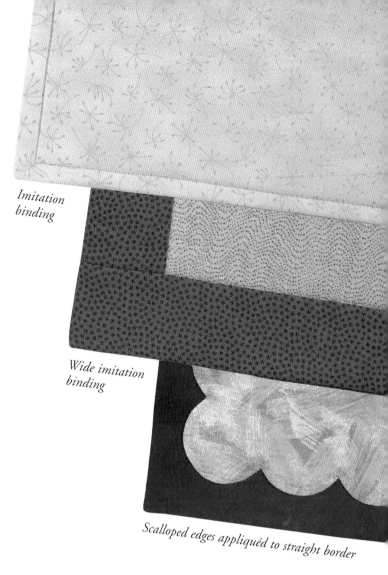

Imitation binding

Wide imitation binding

Scalloped edges appliquéd to straight border

1. Appliqué the curved edges to straight strips of fabric. For a smaller quilt, you could even appliqué the entire quilt top onto a square or rectangle of fabric, and then cut away the excess fabric beneath the quilt top.
2. Sew the front and the back of the quilt together along the straight edges. Attach batting, trim, and turn right side out.
3. Quilt in the ditch along the appliqué curves for a very special quilt finish.

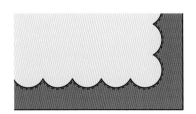

Working with Sculpted Edges

Sculpted edges feature curves and angles that flow around the edge of the quilt. To keep these edges from stretching, do not trim the backing fabric until the edges have been stitched.

1. Cut the backing at least 2" larger than the quilt top, but keep the edges straight. Place the front and back of the quilt right sides together, with the quilt top on top. Pin the edges.

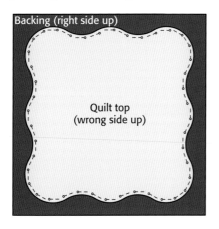

Backing (right side up)

Quilt top
(wrong side up)

2. Sew a ¼" seam around the quilt. Leave an opening on a straight edge (or a gentle curve).

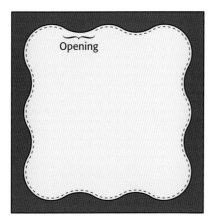

Opening

3. Pin the quilt to the batting and sew the quilt to the batting on the same stitching line.

4. Trim the batting close to the stitching; trim the backing, leaving a ¼" seam allowance. Turn right side out.

5. Hand sew the opening closed. Machine stitch or hand quilt ¼" from the edge to accent the sculpted edges.

Finishing Edges with Backing

*S*ome quilts appear to have binding along the edges but are actually finished by folding the backing fabric to the front, over the batting and quilt top. You can quickly and easily complete a project using this technique.

Finishing your quilt with backing requires that you cut the backing larger than the quilt top. Because most quilters prepare their quilts with the backing already cut longer and wider than the quilt top, you don't need to plan on additional fabric. With this method, the corners can be quickly overlapped or mitered for a finer appearance. In addition to being easy, this technique is an economical way to finish your quilt. You should be aware that edges finished this way, however, are generally not as durable as ones finished with double-fold binding. This method can put more wear and tear on the backing fabric.

That said, using the excess backing fabric to finish the edges is a great method to use if you do not have enough fabric to make binding, as long as your backing fabric coordinates with the quilt design. If not, you may want to reverse the process, turning the quilt-top fabric to the back of the quilt to create the finished edge.

Happy Ending Hint

Think about the use of your quilt when you are considering finishing the edges with the backing. It's great for wall quilts but probably not durable enough for baby quilts or other quilts that will be washed often.

Preparing Your Quilt

1. After quilting your project, lay the quilt on a flat surface and baste around the edges, ¼" from the cut edge of the quilt top. Be sure to stitch through the quilt top, batting, and backing. You can do this by hand or by using a long machine stitch and the walking foot on your machine. This step will keep the layers from shifting as you finish the edges.

2. Use scissors to trim the batting even with the edge of the quilt top, making sure you do *not* cut through the back of the quilt.

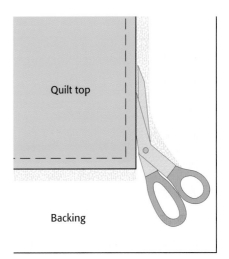

Quilt top

Backing

3. For ½"-wide "binding," you will need 1" of backing fabric extending beyond the edge of the quilt top. Use a rotary ruler to measure 1" of extra fabric around the edges of the quilt top, and trim off the excess fabric with a rotary cutter. If you want "binding" wider than ½", cut the extending fabric two times the desired finished width.

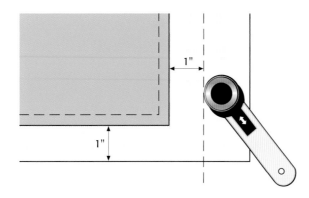

Finishing with Overlapped Corners

1. Fold the 1" of backing fabric in half, wrong sides together, so that the cut edge of the back meets the cut edge of the quilt top.

2. Fold the backing again along the edge of the quilt top to form the finished edge. This fold encases the batting and covers ½" of the quilt top. Pin along the fold to hold the finished edge in place.

3. To finish the corners, extend the fold to the corner.

4. Fold the adjacent side, overlapping the first side at the corners. Pin and then stitch in place.

Happy Ending Hint

Although overlapping the corners is fast and easy, the corners can be bulky and threads of fabric sometimes sneak out of the corner folds. Fold the corners carefully and tuck the raw edges in. Sew the edges closed by hand.

Finishing with Mitered Corners

To improve the appearance of the corners, you can fold a miter. Mitering only takes a few minutes longer, and remember, there are *only* four corners on your quilt! In this method, the corners are folded first, and then the sides.

1. Fold the corner of the backing over the corner point of the quilt top so that the fold touches the point. Make sure you fold the backing squarely over the edge of the quilt.

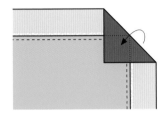

2. Fold the 1" of backing fabric in half, wrong sides together, so that the cut edge of the backing just meets the cut edge of the quilt top.

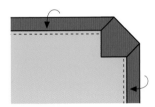

3. Fold the backing once more to create the "binding," and a miter will form at the corner.

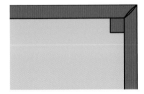

4. Carefully trim the small square that extends onto the quilt. Pin the folds securely and then stitch in place.

Happy Ending Hint

If you get a blunt corner on your finished quilt, try this: Relax! Then, when folding the corner, don't fold the backing fabric tight against the corner of the quilt. Fold it 1/8" outside the point and you'll be able to make a nice, pointed binding corner.

Stitching the Edges

Once your backing edges are folded and pinned, you can stitch them in place by hand or machine.

Finishing by Hand

1. Use an 18" length of thread that matches the backing fabric. Use a blind stitch or a slip stitch to sew the folded edge to the front of the quilt. The stitches should not go all the way through to the back of the quilt.

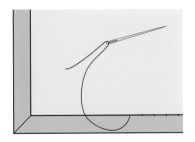

2. At each mitered corner, sew along the mitered fold with four or five stitches, and then continue to sew the next side of the quilt.

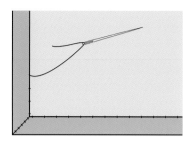

3. After you stitch the backing in place, quilt a row of stitches next to the binding, sewing through all three layers of your quilt to secure the edges and give the illusion of binding on the back of the quilt. Remove any basting stitches.

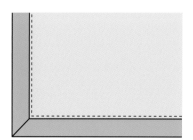

Finishing by Machine

1. To finish the edges by machine, simply sew around the edges of the backing fabric close to the pinned fold. You can use a straight stitch, a machine blind stitch, or a decorative stitch to finish the edges. This stitching sews through all layers of the quilt, so it isn't necessary to add a row of quilting stitches.

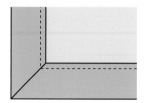 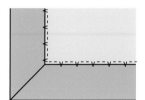

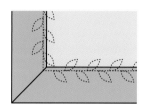

2. Close the overlapped or mitered corners with a few small blind stitches, and then remove any basting stitches.

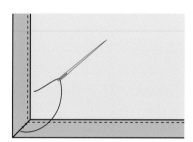

Finishing Edges with Binding

For a more professional finish, you can make a separate binding and apply it to the quilt. You'll need extra fabric to make the binding, so plan ahead and save fabric for this last step. Or you can wait until the quilt is finished and then take it to your favorite quilt shop to audition possible binding fabrics to see which one suits your quilt best.

Applied binding can complement your design by framing the edge of the quilt or matching the background fabric in the design. It can accent a solid border with print binding or simply create a perfect match to your favorite fabric in the quilt. Use a straight or diagonal design in a fabric to create a special binding. Cut fabric with little flowers or hearts printed in a row so that they line up along the edges of your binding. Cut striped fabric so that a single stripe accents your design or so that the stripes spiral around the edge of your quilt. Sew a variety of fabrics together to create a scrappy binding. Unique finishing touches are possible when you make your own binding.

Binding can be cut on the straight grain of your fabric or, when some flexibility is needed to ease around curves, it can be cut on the bias or diagonal grain of the fabric.

Binding can also be applied using various techniques. Single-fold binding works best for some situations, while the more common double-fold binding makes a durable edge finish. These methods, as well as

tips and tricks for finishing irregular edges, are all covered in this chapter.

Applying binding to the edges of a quilt is probably the most common way to finish a quilt today. Making your own binding is both fun and creative.

Following are some options for choosing the right fabric for your binding:

- Choose binding fabrics that complement the design and color in your quilt.

- Use a darker color to frame your quilt and accent the design.

- Use an unusual color to add pizzazz to the quilt edge.

- Avoid lighter colors because they tend to make the edges of the quilt fade away, unless, of course, your border fabric is also light.

- Cut plaid or striped fabrics on the bias to make the most of the design. Stripes also work nicely when they are cut so that the stripes run horizontally around the quilt.

In addition to color and pattern, you'll need to make some other decisions about the type of binding you're going to use. Let's review the pros and cons of single-fold versus double-fold bindings, and straight-grain versus bias binding. Once you decide what type of binding you want to add, you can easily calculate how much fabric you need and how to cut it.

Single-Fold versus Double-Fold Binding

Single-fold binding, which is sometimes referred to as traditional binding, covers the edges of the quilt with one layer of fabric. Double-fold, or French, binding, covers the edges of the quilt with two layers of fabric, making it more durable. Most quilt-pattern instructions call for double-fold binding because of its durability; however, there are occasions when you might want the flexibility of using a single-fold binding. For instance, when you bind irregular edges, such as on a Grandmother's Flower Garden quilt, you'll find it easier to maneuver all the angles if you're using just a single layer of binding fabric. For most other situations, however, double-fold binding is more desirable. The illustrations below show the difference in how the fabric covers the quilt edges with the two types of bindings.

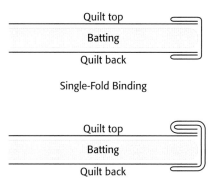

Single-Fold Binding

Double-Fold Binding

Straight-Grain versus Bias Binding

In addition to determining how many layers of fabric you want in your binding, you'll also need to decide if you want or need to use bias or straight-grain binding. Cutting your binding strips on the straight of grain is quick and easy to do, and it requires less fabric than bias binding. It works very nicely for quilts with straight edges and square corners.

However, if your quilt has curved edges, rounded corners, or unusual shaped angles, bias binding is the best option. Cutting the fabric on the bias (at a 45° angle to the selvage edge) gives your strips a built-in stretch that helps your binding round the curves and still lie smoothly. Bias binding also miters quite nicely at the corners. When applied to the edge of your quilt, the bias threads cross the edge, creating a durable finish.

Of course, you can also use bias binding on a quilt with straight edges to take advantage of the binding-fabric design. Stripes and plaids look great made into bias binding because the design lines fall on the diagonal, creating a wraparound effect at the edges. Even some print fabrics that have a linear design create a nicer binding when cut on the bias.

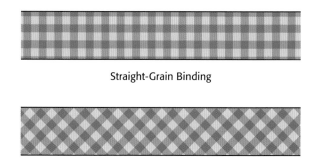

Straight-Grain Binding

Bias Binding

Determining Yardage for Binding

Armed with your decision about what type of binding you'll make, whether it's single-fold bias binding or straight-grain double-fold binding, and the size quilt you're making, you can now use that information to help you determine how much binding you'll need and ultimately how much fabric you'll need to buy.

How Many Binding Strips Are Needed?
Start by calculating how many inches of binding you'll need to go around the perimeter of your quilt. Many project directions may provide this information for you, but it's easy enough to calculate yourself, especially if you have a calculator handy! Simply measure around the outside edges of your quilt and add about 10" extra for seam allowances and turning the corners. (If your quilt has scalloped or sculpted edges, measure around the curved edges using a flexible tape measure.)

Instead of measuring all the way around your quilt, you can measure the length and the width, add the two measurements together, and multiply the answer by two. Then add 10" extra. For instance, if you're making a crib quilt that measures 45" x 60", add 45 + 65 = 110; 110 x 2 = 220; 220 + 10 = 230. You'll need 230" of binding.

If you are planning straight-grain binding, divide 230" by the width of your fabric. I use 42" fabric, but to allow for seam allowances and shrinkage, I divide the total inches needed by 40". In this example, 230 ÷ 40 = 5.75. Round that up to the next whole number, and you'll see that you need to cut six binding strips for your quilt.

For bias binding, each strip is a different length, so you'll have to measure the strips as you cut them to see how many total strips you'll need to make 230" of binding.

How Wide Will Your Strips Be?
The second piece of information you'll need to determine how much fabric it will take to bind your quilt is how wide you will cut your strips. The answer to that question again depends on what type of binding you've decided to make.

Single-fold binding. This option covers the edge with a single layer of fabric and finishes approximately one-quarter of the width of the cut-size strip.

Traditional binding cut 2" wide allows for two ½" seam allowances, with ½" showing on the front of the quilt and ½" showing on the back. (I like to use ½" seams on single-fold binding because it's easier to control the fabric while stitching—especially with bias strips.) If you cut 2½"-wide binding strips, you will have a finished size of ⅝"; 3"-wide strips finish at ¾". If you are using thick batting, add ¼" to the cut size to allow the binding to turn over the thickness of the batting.

Note that this technique works fine on quilts with wide borders, but if patchwork blocks or pieced borders go right to the edges of the quilt, the wide seam allowance will bite into the patchwork design, cutting off any points.

Double-fold binding. This option applies a double layer of fabric around the quilt edges and finishes to approximately one-sixth the width of the cut-strip size. For example, double-fold binding cut 2" wide allows for two ¼" seam allowances and ⅜" showing on the front and back of the quilt, with ⅜" for the front and back of the quilt on the inside layer. If you'd like a wider binding, you can cut 2½"-wide strips, and the finished size will be ½", using ¼" seam allowances. If you use a thick batting in your quilt, it's a good idea to add ¼" to the cut size to allow for the batting thickness.

Mimi's Favorite

I like to cut binding strips 2" wide for double-fold binding. This started with my first rotary ruler, which was only 2" wide. But seriously, I like this size because finished double-fold binding sews on smoothly with a ¼" seam allowance, hugs the edge of the quilt, makes a neat miter fold, and covers all stitching when it is turned over the edge of the quilt. I usually use thin batting. For a thicker quilt, I cut the binding 2¼" wide.

Some quilters, however, do prefer wider bindings. You might like a wider frame for your design, or you may feel more comfortable applying a wider strip. Cut wider fabric strips to create wider binding; just remember to account for seam allowances, the binding width on the front and back of your quilt, and the thickness of the quilt.

How Much Fabric Is Needed?
After measuring the distance around your quilt and deciding how wide you want your binding, you can now calculate the amount of fabric you need to make binding. Whether you have full-width yardage or only a square of fabric, the information on page 32 can help you figure out just how much fabric you'll need.

Using a rectangle. Use a rectangle of fabric to easily cut binding strips along the straight grain of the fabric or to cut continuous straight binding (see page 35). You can also use a rectangle of fabric to cut bias strips or continuous bias binding for larger quilts.

Multiply the number of strips needed (see page 30) by the width you want to cut your strips (see page 31). In our crib quilt example, we needed six binding strips. If we want to cut them 2" wide for double-fold binding, we would need 12" of fabric (6 x 2" = 12"). When you buy fabric, allow a little extra for shrinkage or uneven edges. I generally allow ⅛ yard extra when the amount I need is less than a yard. I allow ¼ yard extra when I need more than a yard.

Now you know how to calculate the amount of fabric needed. But for a quick reference, you can put away your calculator and use the following chart as a guide. Fabric amounts are based on 42"-wide fabric.

Quilt sizes are based on standard mattress sizes, with 12" added to the sides, top, and bottom. If you're making a twin-size quilt with 2"-wide cut binding, for example, you'll need at least an 18" length of 42"-wide fabric to cut enough binding.	Standard Quilt Size	Dimensions	Amount of Binding (length plus 10")	Fabric Needed for Strip Width		
				2"	2½"	3"
	Crib	45" x 60"	220"	12"	15"	18"
	Twin	63" x 99"	334"	18"	22½"	27"
	Full	78" x 99"	364"	20"	25"	30"
	Queen	84" x 104"	386"	20"	25"	30"
	King	100" x 104"	418"	22"	27½"	33"

Using a square. If you don't have full-width yardage of your binding fabric, you can also use a square to cut strips or continuous straight binding.

1. To determine the size of the square needed, multiply the length of binding you need by the width of your cut binding to calculate the total number of square inches of fabric needed to make your binding. Example:

    For a 45" x 60" crib quilt with 2" binding
    Length of binding = 210" plus 10" = 220"
    220" x 2" = 440"

2. Find the square root of the number of square inches needed. (Don't faint—just enter the number of square inches into your calculator and press the square-root button for the answer!) Round off this number to the next highest *even* number to allow extra for seam allowances.

    Square root of 440 = 20.97". Round up to 22". This is the size of the fabric square you will need to cut enough binding. Below you'll find a quick reference chart for standard-size quilts, just in case you don't want to do the math.

Quilt sizes are based on standard mattress sizes, with 12" added to the sides, top, and bottom. If you're making a full-size quilt with 2"-wide cut binding, you'll need at least a 28" square of fabric to cut enough binding.	Standard Quilt Size	Dimensions	Amount of Binding (length plus 10")	Square Needed for Strip Width		
				2"	2½"	3"
	Crib	45" x 60"	220"	22"	24"	26"
	Twin	63" x 99"	334"	26"	30"	32"
	Full	78" x 99"	364"	28"	32"	36"
	Queen	84" x 104"	386"	30"	34"	36"
	King	100" x 104"	418"	32"	36"	38"

Cutting Binding Strips

Whether you're making straight-grain or bias binding, the strips are easy to cut with a rotary cutter and ruler. Always prewash your fabric when you are making your own binding to prevent it from shrinking and puckering after it is applied to your quilt.

Straight-Grain Strips

Cutting straight-grain binding strips is as simple as cutting strips for any other part of your patchwork quilt. Simply cut strips straight across the width or length of your fabric, taking care to fold the fabric accurately so that your strips will be straight when the fold is opened up. You can also cut straight-grain binding with the continuous method on page 35.

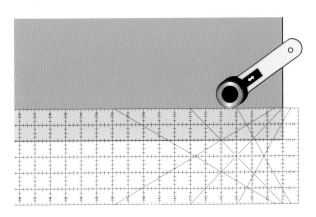

Bias Strips

Bias binding is cut on the diagonal grain of the fabric. Make bias binding by cutting separate diagonal strips of fabric or by using the continuous method described on page 36.

1. Starting in one corner of your fabric next to a selvage edge, use a ruler to make a mark 6" from each side of the corner. Using your rotary ruler, connect these marks and cut off the corner triangle of fabric.

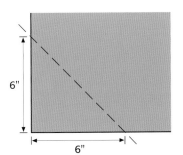

2. Move the ruler over so that the 2" line is aligned with the first cut. Cut along the edge of the ruler to make your first bias strip. Continue cutting 2"-wide strips this way until you have enough binding strips to go around the edges of your quilt.

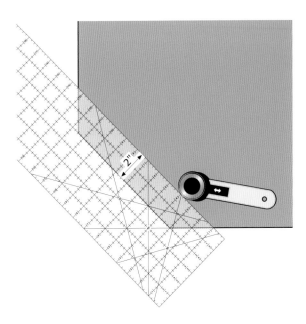

Cutting Quick Bias Strips

1. Fold a fabric square in half diagonally and press. Fold the square a second time and press.

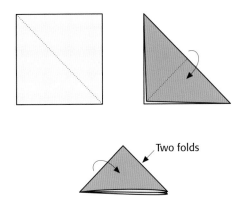

Two folds

2. Make a clean cut along the edge with the two folds to remove them. Cut 2"-wide strips parallel to the cut edge.

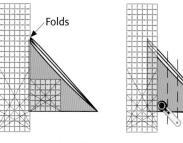

Remove both folds.　　　Cut bias strips.

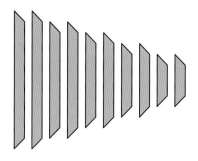

Sewing Binding Strips Together

Once your binding strips are cut, you'll need to sew them together into one long strip. The total length of the joined strips should be longer than the distance around your quilt to allow for turning the corners and joining the two ends.

The easiest way to sew the straight-grain strips together is to connect the pieces using straight seams; however, this method creates bulky areas when folded and stitched as binding. To make a binding that will lie flat and smooth even where there are seams, it's best to sew the strips together with diagonal seams.

Diagonal seams in binding improve the finished look of your project. When the binding is folded over the edge of the quilt, the bulk of the seam is distributed in opposite directions. On bias binding, using a diagonal seam means you're stitching along the straight of grain, so it prevents the seam from stretching.

Joining Bias Strips

By their very nature, strips you cut on the bias will have ends that are angled at 45° to the length of the strip. (You can also cut straight-grain strips so that their ends are angled for this sewing method.)

1. Place two binding strips right sides together with the diagonal edges aligned. Slide them so that the ends extend ¼".

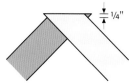

2. Sew a ¼" seam across the cut edges.

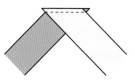

3. Press the seam open and trim off the part of the seam allowance that extends beyond the edge of the binding. This will help reduce bulk in the finished binding.

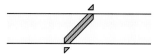

4. Continue adding strips in the same manner until you have enough binding to go around your quilt, plus 10".

Joining Straight-Grain Strips

1. Place two strips right sides together, crossing the ends at right angles. Lay them on a flat surface and pin securely.

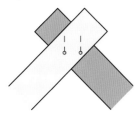

2. Imagine the strips as the capital letter *A*. Draw a line across the pieces to connect the points where they intersect, just like crossing the *A*, and then sew along the line.

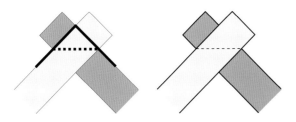

3. Trim the excess fabric, leaving a ¼" seam allowance, and press the seams open.

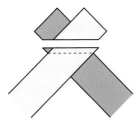

4. Continue adding strips in the same manner until you have enough binding to go around your quilt, plus 10".

Cutting Continuous Binding

Some quilters like the continuous binding method, which allows you to start with a large piece of fabric, sew one or two seams, and then do the cutting. The result is one long (continuous) piece of binding. It eliminates the process of sewing many separate strips together. You can use this method for both straight-grain and bias binding.

Continuous Straight-Grain Binding

For this method, you sew only one seam, and then cut one long, continuous binding strip. It takes time to mark the cutting lines, but if you don't like sewing many individual strips together, this method may be for you. Because this binding is cut on the straight grain of the fabric, it should be used only to bind quilts with straight edges and square corners.

1. Using one of the charts on page 32, determine the rectangle or square size that will yield enough binding for your project.

2. Lay your fabric on a flat surface, and trim off any selvages. Mark lines 2" apart, parallel to one long edge. If the fabric beyond the last line measures less than 2" wide, trim it off. (You shouldn't have to trim if the measurement of the fabric can be divided by your binding width).

3. Place side A and side B right sides together. Shift side A so that the top cut edge of side A matches up with the first line marked on side B. At the other end of the seam, the lower cut edge of side B should match the last line on side A. Pin in place and then sew a ¼" seam. It's good to use a smaller-than-normal stitch length (about 12 to 15 stitches per inch) since you'll be cutting through the seam. Press the seam open.

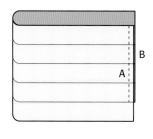

4. Using sharp scissors, start at one uneven end and cut along the marked line. When you get to the seam, you will have moved up one line and can continue to cut one piece of binding long enough to bind your quilt.

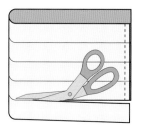

Continuous Bias Binding

This method is similar to the continuous straight-grain binding in that you mark and sew first, and then cut one long piece of continuous binding. In this case, the binding is cut on the bias, making it suitable for any finishing situation, including curved or scalloped edges as well as rounded or mitered corners.

1. Using one of the charts on page 32, determine the square or rectangle size that will yield enough binding for your project.

2. Lay your fabric on a flat surface, right side up, and label the sides A, B, C, and D as shown. Use a water-soluble pen or write on masking tape.

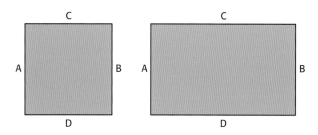

3. If you are using a square, fold the square in half diagonally and press lightly. Cut along this fold to create two triangles. Place sides A and B right sides together as shown so that the points where the triangles intersect are ¼" from the cut edges. Sew the triangles together using a ¼" seam allowance and a stitch length of 12 to 15 stitches per inch. Press the seam open.

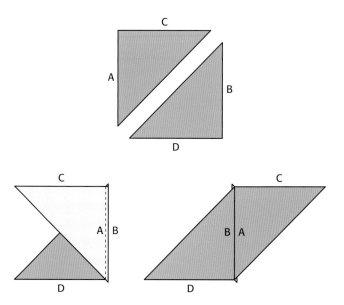

If you are using a rectangle, fold side A down to match side D. Press this diagonal fold lightly and cut along the fold line to create the bias edges.

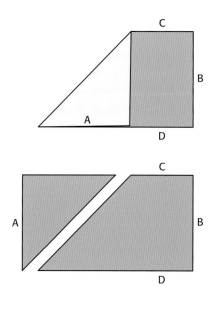

4. Place sides A and B right sides together and sew a ¼" seam, using 12 to 15 stitches per inch. Press the seam open and place the fabric on a flat surface.

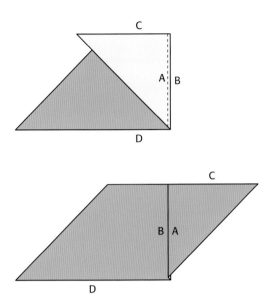

5. Whether you started with a square or a rectangle, you now have a parallelogram. For either piece, start on one unmarked side and draw a parallel line 2" (the binding width) from the bias edge. Continue drawing parallel lines 2" apart across the whole piece of fabric. Be careful not to stretch your fabric as you draw the lines. Trim off the fabric at the end if it is less than 2".

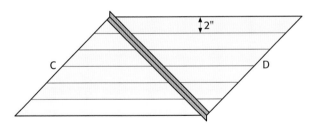

6. Bring sides C and D right sides together to create a tube of fabric. Shift one edge of C so that it matches the first line marked on D. At the other end, the end of D will match the last line on C. Pin the edges together and then stitch a ¼" seam. It may seem a little awkward because the fabric

will not lie flat. Don't worry; that means you've aligned it correctly! Press the seam open.

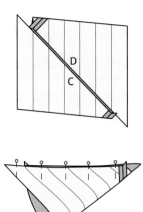

7. Using scissors and beginning at one uneven end, start cutting along the marked line. When you get to the seam, you will have moved down one line and can continue to cut enough binding for your quilt.

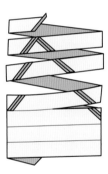

Cut along lines to form a continuous strip.

Happy Ending Hint

When making continuous binding for a large quilt, place the binding tube over your ironing board. Keep turning the tube of fabric as you cut the binding.

Cutting Special Fabrics for Bindings

Fabrics with small, evenly spaced designs can create very special bindings for your quilt. Designs repeated in straight or diagonal patterns can be cut into straight or bias strips to highlight the printed design in the binding. A row of small flowers or hearts can be lined up along the edge of your quilt to add the perfect touch.

Plaids and stripes also make terrific bindings. You can cut them on the straight of grain or on the bias, depending on the look you'd like for your quilt.

Small Prints

If you'd like to have the print design show evenly on both the front and back of your quilt, you'll have to plan how to cut your strips, rather than just cut one 2"-wide strip after the other. You may need to trim off some of the fabric before cutting the next binding strip so that you can center the design as needed.

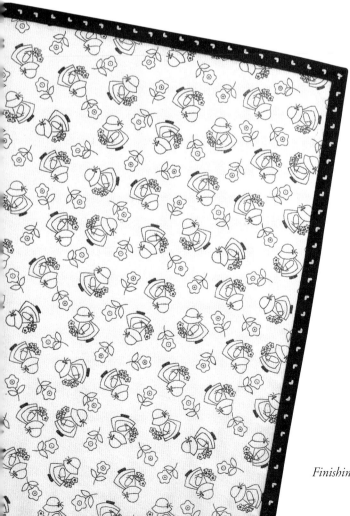

For single-fold binding, you'll need to have four repeats of the design to have finished binding with a single row of motifs on the front and on the back. (Remember, the edges will be taken up in the seam allowances.)

For double-fold binding, you'll need to have six repeats of the design for one row to show on the front and one row on the back. That's because with double-fold binding the finished binding width is roughly one-sixth of the cut size.

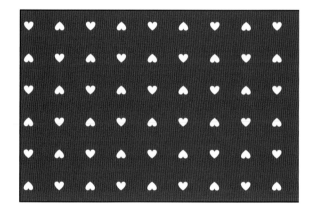

You may need to adjust your binding width to accommodate enough designs. Cut strips of fabric to make enough binding for your quilt, each strip having the same rows of designs. The strips can be cut on the straight grain or on the bias, depending on the design in the fabric. Some diagonal designs may not be printed on a true bias, but your binding will look beautiful if you apply it carefully. Sew the strips together according to the directions on page 35, and you will have a very special binding for your quilt.

Striped Binding

Striped fabric can be used in three different ways to accent the edges of your quilt.

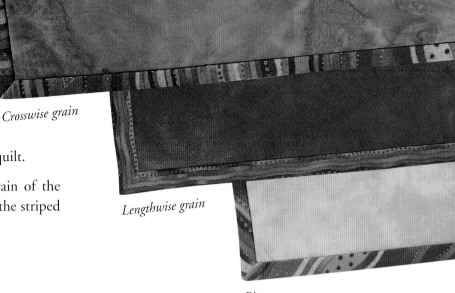

Crosswise grain

Lengthwise grain

Bias

🔘 Strips cut on the crosswise straight grain of the fabric will show all colors and parts of the striped design when sewn to your quilt.

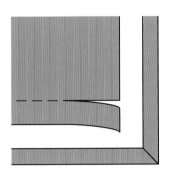

🔘 Strips cut parallel to the lengthwise straight grain of the fabric will show a particular section of the striped design. When all strips are cut identically, you can use them to create a frame around your quilt.

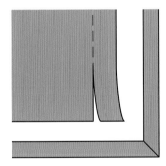

🔘 Strips cut on the bias will create diagonal stripes that spiral around the edge of your quilt.

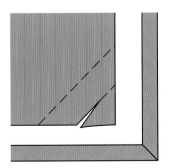

Plaid Binding

Like striped fabric, you can cut plaid binding on the straight of grain to feature a particular segment of the plaid, or you can cut it on the bias so that the entire design will be seen as it wraps diagonally around the edges of your quilt.

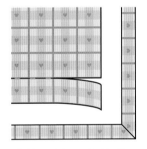 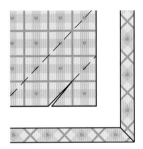

Plaid straight-grain binding   Plaid bias binding

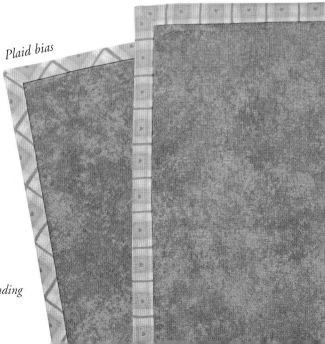

Plaid straight grain

Plaid bias

Straight-grain binding   *Bias binding*

Cutting Scrappy Binding

Piece together fabrics from your quilt design to make a unique patchwork binding. As you finish your scrappy binding with hand stitches, choose a thread color that blends with a medium color in your binding or matches the back of the quilt. One way to make a scrappy binding is to start with a strip set. The other way is to sew individual strips together end to end. The first method makes smaller individual pieces while the second gives you longer strips of each fabric.

Strip-Set Method

You can cut straight-grain or bias strips for the strip-set method.

Straight-Grain Binding

1. Sew strips of the various fabrics together lengthwise to make a strip set. You can cut all strips the same width or mix and match for a truly random binding. Use a short stitch length, about 15 to 20 stitches per inch, to sew the strips together. The short stitches will hold the little pieces securely when you crosscut the strip sets. Press the seam allowances open to distribute the thickness of the seams along the binding edge.

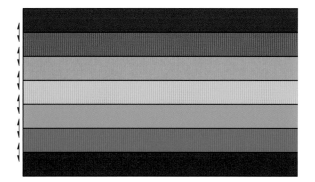

2. Use a rotary cutter and a ruler to clean-cut the edges of the strip set. Crosscut the strip to make patchwork strips the width of your desired binding. **Note:** It's best to cut scrappy binding ¼" wider than usual to allow for the thickness of all the seams around the quilt edge.

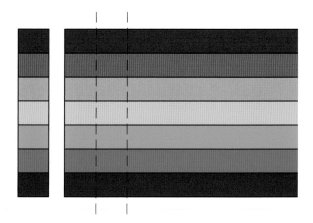

3. Sew the strip-set segments together end to end to make enough binding to go around your quilt.

Bias Binding

Cutting the strip set on the diagonal will give your scrappy binding a spiral or candy cane effect.

1. Cut strips on the straight of grain and then sew them together in a stair-step fashion. Each time you add a new strip to the strip set, move the end down the width of the cut strip.

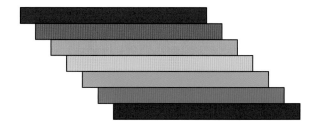

2. Place a long rotary-cutting ruler along the diagonal stair-step edge and use a rotary cutter to cut binding strips the desired width. Be sure to align the 45° line on the ruler with one of the seam lines in the strip set so that your binding will be cut on the true bias.

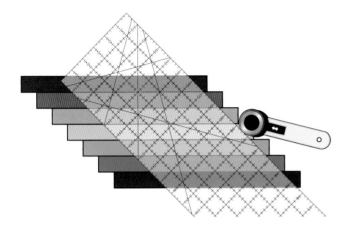

3. Join the strip-set segments end to end to make binding long enough to go around your quilt.

Individual-Strips Method

An easy way to incorporate leftovers from your quilt top into binding is to cut individual strips from each of the fabrics you want to use. (Maybe you even have some leftover strips already cut.) Simply sew these strips together end to end, using a diagonal seam as described on page 35. Unlike the strip-set method, your binding will have longer lengths of each color fabric and fewer seams along the way. This type of binding requires no more effort than typical double-fold binding; you're just substituting several colors for the typical single-color binding.

Applying Binding to a Quilt

Now that you've determined what type of binding you want to make, what fabric you want to use, and how to cut the strips and sew them together, you're ready to attach the binding to your quilt. It pays to prepare the quilt edges neatly before sewing. Then you can follow the steps for applying the binding, mitering the corners, and finishing the binding.

Note: If you plan to add a hanging sleeve to your quilt, you may want to do so before adding the binding. See "Hanging Sleeves" on page 68.

Preparing the Quilt for Binding

It is very important to baste the quilt edges together before attaching the binding so that the quilt top, batting, and backing can be treated as one unit. Basting stitches also stabilize the edge of the quilt to prevent stretching. It's also important to prepare the quilt edges so that the batting will extend to the edge of the binding to fill it and give it body along the quilt edges.

Mimi's Favorite

I always machine baste around the edges of the three quilt layers before binding. It's much easier to sew the binding to one quilt than to three separate layers.

Here's how to baste your quilt edges:
1. Place your quilted project on a flat surface and smooth out the top, batting, and backing. The quilt top should be face up.
2. Pin the layers securely around the edges, placing straight pins about 3" apart through all layers.
3. Using a walking foot or an even-feed foot (see page 11) and a long stitch on your sewing machine, baste ⅛" from the cut edge of the quilt top. Be careful that the layers don't shift. (If you wish, you can baste the edges by hand.)

4. Use a rotary cutter and a ruler to trim the batting, backing, and any excess threads even with the quilt top to create a clean edge on your quilt so that you are ready to apply the binding. **Note:** If you're using wider binding, you may need to trim the batting ¼" or so away from the edge of the quilt so that you'll have enough batting to fill out the folded binding.

5. Use a 6" x 12" or 6"-square ruler to make sure that the corners are square. Trim if necessary.

Happy Ending Hint

Check the opposite sides of your quilt to make sure they are the same length. You can adjust the length of the quilt edges by tightening or loosening the basting stitches.

Using a Walking Foot

A walking foot, which is sometimes called an even-feed foot, is a sewing-machine attachment or built-in feature that helps feed the quilt layers under the needle at the same pace. This foot helps keep the quilt smooth and prevents the layers from shifting and puckering.

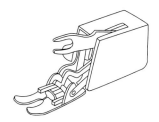

Walking or Even-Feed Foot

Many quilters measure the ¼" seam allowance as they sew by aligning the fabric edge with the edge of the presser foot. A walking foot is typically wider than a ¼" patchwork foot, so if you use it as a guide, your seam may be too wide. To avoid this problem, you

may be able to adjust the needle position on your machine by moving the needle slightly to the right. If that's not an option on your machine, you can place a piece of masking tape on your machine to mark the ¼" seam allowance and guide the fabric edge along the tape. Test the seam allowance on a scrap of fabric before sewing the binding to your quilt.

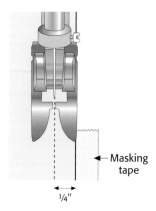

← Masking tape

¼"

Getting Started

Before you sew the binding to your quilt, take a moment to think about the starting point.

- Start sewing in a corner only if you are planning to overlap the corners or sew the miters. (See page 49 for "Stitched Mitered Corners.") It's much easier to make a folded miter in a corner than to sew the miter together there.

- If your quilt has rounded corners, start on a straight edge rather than on a curve.

- Avoid starting to sew the binding exactly in the middle of a quilt edge. Each time you fold your quilt in half, it will weaken at that spot.

So where's the best place to begin sewing the binding? Somewhere between the corner and the center of a side. On a large quilt, it may not matter where you start, but on a small wall hanging, you should choose a starting point that will not show later, such as the top edge.

Happy Ending Hints

- Do not pin the binding to the entire quilt before sewing. As you sew, the binding may "bubble up" between the pins and cause little tucks. It's also very uncomfortable to sew with all of those pins sticking you.

- As you sew, concentrate on the 3" of binding directly in front of the sewing-machine needle. Lay the first 3" in position and sew; then go on to the next 3". Before long, these 3" lengths will add up to the entire quilt!

- Be careful not to stretch your binding as you sew. Keep the long piece of binding in your lap, rather than letting it fall to the floor.

- Support the weight of the quilt on a table to the left of your sewing machine.

- Use a long straight pin or stiletto to control the layers in front of the presser foot and needle as you sew. It's a lot safer than sticking your finger in harm's way, and besides, a pin or stiletto fits much better than your finger.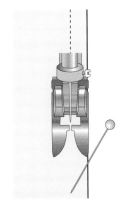

- Your binding can also be stitched to the edge of the quilt by hand. Use a small running stitch to sew the binding to the three quilt layers. Add a backstitch every 2" to secure your stitches.

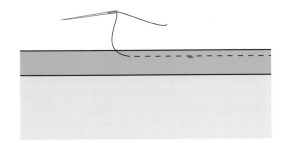

1. Place one end of the binding 6" from one of the corners. Align the cut edges of the binding strip with the cut edges of the quilt.

2. Using a walking foot or an even-feed foot, start sewing 4" from the beginning of the binding. Use a ¼" seam allowance and a stitch length of 10 stitches per inch. You do not need to backstitch when you begin to attach the binding.

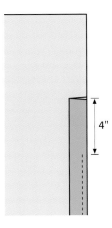

Applying Single-Fold Binding to Straight Edges

Single-fold binding requires a ½"-wide seam allowance and works well on wide borders. Do not use this binding if the quilt features pieced borders or patchwork that extends to the edges of the quilt.

1. Press the binding strip in half lengthwise, wrong sides together.

2. Fold each cut edge toward the fold and press again.

3. Open the folds of the binding and place the binding, right sides together, along the edge of the quilt. Align one cut edge of the binding to the raw edge of the quilt.

4. Sew through all layers with a ½" seam allowance, using the fold as a guide.

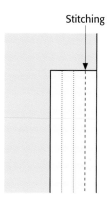

5. Fold the binding over the edge of the quilt to cover the raw edges and the seam allowance on the back of the quilt. The second fold of the binding should cover the stitching on the back of the quilt. You can trim the quilt edge slightly if the binding is not wide enough to cover the stitches.

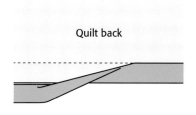

6. Sew the pressed edge of the binding to the back of the quilt by hand, using a blind stitch or slip stitch.

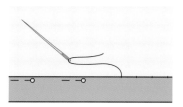

Single-fold binding can also be finished completely by machine. Sew the binding strip to the *back* side of the quilt first. When it is turned to the front of the quilt, stitch by machine along the pressed fold of the binding. For this very quick method of applying binding, refer to "Machine-Finished Binding" in "Stitching Guide" on page 75.

Applying Double-Fold Binding to Straight Edges

1. Fold the binding strip in half lengthwise, wrong sides together. Press the folded strip with a steam iron to help the two layers stay together as you sew. You can also use spray starch.

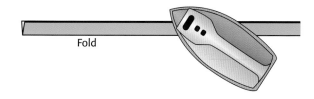

2. Match the two cut edges of the binding to the cut edge of the quilt. Sew the binding to the quilt with a ¼" seam.

3. Fold the binding over the edge of the quilt to the back. The folded edge of the binding should cover

the stitching on the back of the quilt. You can trim the quilt edge slightly if the binding will not cover the seam.

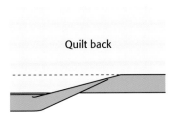

Quilt back

4. Hand stitch the folded edge of the binding to the back of the quilt, using a blind stitch or slip stitch.

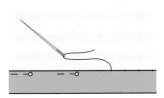

Double-fold binding can also be finished completely by machine. Sew the binding strip to the *back* of the quilt first, and then turn the folded edge to the front. Sew along the folded edge with the sewing machine. For this very quick method of applying binding, refer to "Machine-Finished Binding" in "Stitching Guide."

Quilt top

Happy Ending Hint

When folding binding in half, match the two cut edges, but let the bottom layer extend slightly. You don't need to measure this distance; you just want to be able to see the bottom layer. When you sew the binding to your quilt, you will be able to *see* both layers and will be in control if one shifts or unfolds. Try it on your next quilt!

Finishing Corners

Quilts generally have four corners that need binding. You can overlap individual strips of binding at the corners, make folded or stitched miters at the corners, or round the quilt corners off first and then use bias binding to turn the curves. Each of these techniques is explained in this section.

Rounded Corners

Rounding off the corners of your quilt allows you to apply the binding without stopping to miter the binding at the corners. Take a good look at the design of your quilt. If it has wide borders or wide areas of background fabric in the corners, you can round off the corners. However, if there is a very definite square pattern in the corner, your quilt will look better if you keep the corners intact and miter the binding. *Important:* You must cut your binding on the bias so that it will stretch around the curves.

1. Mark the rounded corner with a pencil so that the circle touches adjacent sides of the quilt. Repeat for all four corners. You can round the quilt corners easily by using a round dish as explained on page 22.

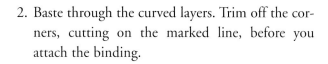

2. Baste through the curved layers. Trim off the corners, cutting on the marked line, before you attach the binding.

3. As you apply the binding around the curve, do not stretch the binding. If the binding is stretched, the corner will not lie flat when the binding is finished. Do not clip the binding to get it to go around the curve. As you place it around the curve, gently ease the binding fabric so that it matches the seam line on the quilt. This will allow the binding to lie flat when you fold it over the quilt edge.

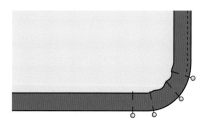

Folded Mitered Corners

For quilts with square corners, folding the binding to miter the corner is one of the easiest ways to create a professional finish to your binding. It only takes a few minutes to fold the miters in the corners, and they provide the perfect accent to many quilts. Small quilts, wall hangings, quilts with narrow borders, and quilts with square designs in the corners look especially nice with mitered corners. You can make mitered corners using straight-grain or bias binding. Remember, there are only four corners on a quilt. You'll be an expert by the third one!

1. Sew the binding along the first edge of the quilt. If you are using double-fold binding, stop stitching ¼" from the end and backstitch. If you are using single-fold binding or if your seam allowance is wider than ¼", you will need to stop stitching the width of the seam from the end.

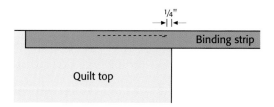

Happy Ending Hint

Use a long straight pin to ease the binding under the presser foot on your sewing machine. You can also pin the binding around the curve before you sew.

Happy Ending Hint

A straight pin will help you mark the place to stop stitching. Turn your quilt to the wrong side and stick a pin into the corner so that it is ¼" from each of the edges, pushing it straight through all layers. The place where the pin comes out on the top marks the place where you will stop stitching. Insert another pin in this spot on the front and pin the binding to the quilt. "Where the pin goes in" signals your place to stop stitching.

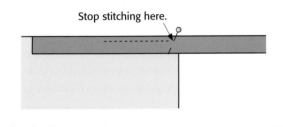

Stop stitching here.

2. Fold the binding so that it extends straight up from the second edge of the quilt. You'll be creating a diagonal fold, which will in turn create the miter.

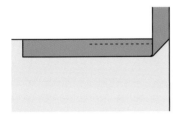

3. Fold the binding down, aligning it with the second edge of the quilt. The fold should be even with the first edge of the quilt. You may want to use a couple of pins to hold the fold in place.

Fold.

4. Sew the binding to the next edge of the quilt. You can start right at the edge unless your machine has a hard time getting started on so many layers of fabric. In that case, you can start sewing ¼" from the fold, but make sure to backstitch.

5. Repeat these steps for the remaining corners on your quilt.

Happy Ending Hint

If it looks as though a binding seam will occur near the miter fold, you can choose to ignore it and live with a little bulk. If you prefer, remove the quilt from the sewing machine and reseam the binding so that the seam falls before the mitered corner.

6. To complete the binding, you'll need to fold the miters on the front and the back. On the quilt top, place your finger under the corner fold and push the fabric toward the point.

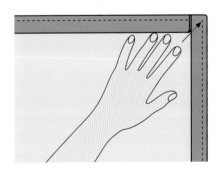

7. Fold the binding over the edge and toward the back of the quilt. On the front, the fabric automatically folds into a miter.

8. On the back, fold the binding flat over one edge of the quilt. At the corner, the binding will form a diagonal fold. As you turn under the second edge, the diagonal fold creates a miter on the back of the quilt.

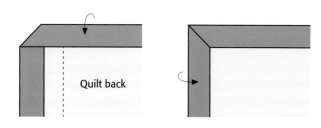

Quilt back

9. Hand stitch the binding to the back of the quilt, taking three or four blind stitches along the mitered fold on the back. Then stick the needle through to the front and take three or four stitches along the miter on the front. Push the needle through to the back of the quilt and continue stitching the binding onto the back of the quilt.

Happy Ending Hint

As you fold the binding to the back, work from the back of the quilt and fold one edge first, and then continue around the quilt counterclockwise to fold the other edges. This way, the miters on the back will be folded with the bulk going in the opposite direction of the miters on the top of the quilt, thereby distributing the fabric thickness at each corner.

Folded Miters for Other Angles

The folded-miter method can be used on angles that are not square, such as on vests or six- or eight-sided quilts.

1. Stitch the binding to the first side of the quilt, stopping ¼" (or the width of the seam) from the first angle, and backstitch.

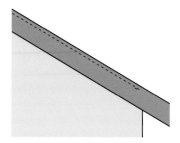

2. As you make the first binding fold, make sure that the binding strip extends so that it is in line with the second edge of the quilt as shown.

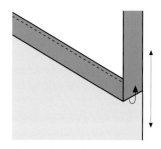

3. Fold the binding down so that it is aligned with the second edge of the quilt. Note that the folded edge will not be in line with the first edge of the quilt as it is for square-corner quilts. However, the fold should still touch the first side at the point, creating a small tuck as you continue stitching the binding.

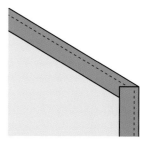

4. To finish the binding, fold it to the back and hand stitch it in place as in steps 6–9 beginning on page 47.

Stitched Mitered Corners

While folding mitered corners is a bit quicker and easier than stitching the miters at each corner, this technique is a handy one to know for the times when you'd like different-colored binding on adjoining sides of your quilt. You can still have the professional look of a mitered corner, but have two different fabrics coming together to create the miter.

Straight-grain binding is easier to control for this technique than bias binding. Cut each binding strip so that it is 4" longer than the quilt side. As you place your binding on the edge of the quilt, allow 2" to extend beyond each end of the quilt.

1. Sew a binding strip to each side of the quilt, stopping ¼" from the ends (or the width of your binding seam), and backstitch.

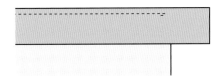

2. Fold the binding out over the seam allowances, overlapping the two strips at right angles. If you are applying single-fold binding, fold the second seam allowance now. Mark the strips where they cross (point A in the diagram).

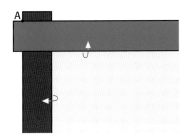

3. On the wrong side of the binding, draw a line from point A into the corner seam (point B). Then place your ruler along the stitching line and make a mark at the folded edge of the binding, directly across from the corner seam, at point C.

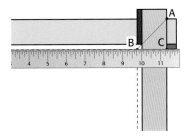

4. Place your ruler so that it is perpendicular to the drawn A-B line and touches point C and the diagonal line. Draw a line from point C to the A-B line to create point D.

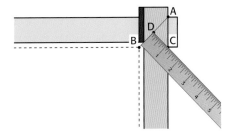

5. Fold the quilt top with right sides together so that the two binding strips are aligned and the A points match.

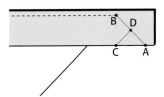

6. Sew from B to D, pivot, and then stitch from D to C. Trim the seam allowance to ¼" and finger-press it open.

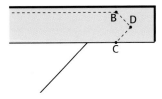

7. Fold the binding over the edge of the quilt, forming miters on the front and back. Hand stitch the folded edge of the binding to the back of the quilt, using a blind stitch or slip stitch.

Quilt back

Overlapped Corners

Binding can be applied to each side of the quilt separately and overlapped at the corners instead of mitering the corners. This type of binding is common on Amish quilts. You can make overlapped corners with straight-grain or bias binding. Use this technique only with single-fold (traditional) binding; double-fold binding may be too thick. Cut binding strips 4" longer than the quilt sides to allow extra fabric for overlapping at the corners.

1. Sew binding strips to two opposite sides of the quilt, stitching from one cut edge to the other.

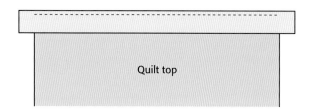

2. Fold the binding over the edge and hand sew the binding to the back of your quilt. Trim off the excess fabric at each end.

3. Sew binding onto the other two sides of the quilt, overlapping the first two binding strips as shown. Trim the ends of the binding, leaving ¼" of binding beyond each end of the quilt.

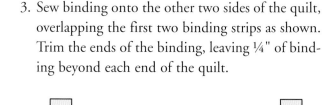

4. Fold the cut ends of the binding to the wrong side so that the fold is even with the first binding strips. Then fold the binding to the back of the quilt, enclosing all the cut edges.

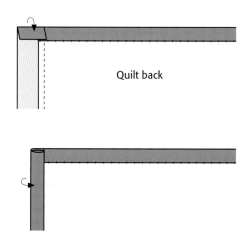

5. Using a blind stitch, sew the folded edge of the binding to the back of the quilt and stitch the corners closed.

Connecting the Binding Ends

When you have stitched the binding to the back of the quilt and returned to the starting place, you have a few options to connect the starting and finishing ends of the binding. You can sew the binding pieces together with a straight seam, but that method creates unsightly bulk. This method is probably the best choice only if you've made scrappy binding with straight seams (see page 40). Making a diagonal connection is a better choice if you've used diagonal seams for all the other joins in your binding strips. A lot of quilters simply fold under one end of the binding and tuck the other end inside to make a diagonal connection. If that's how you currently finish your binding, try Mimi's Favorite quick-and-easy method on page 52 to make a smoother finish.

Straight Connections

Use this method only if the other seams in your binding strips are sewn perpendicular to the length of binding and you want the connection to look just like all the other seams.

1. Stop sewing the binding approximately 4" away from the starting point. Cut the end of your binding with a straight cut so that it overlaps the beginning end of the binding by ½".

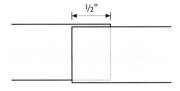

2. Unfold the two ends of the binding and place them right sides together. Sew the ends together with a ¼" seam allowance. Press the seam open to distribute the thickness.

3. Refold the seamed section of the strip, return it to the edge of the quilt, and finish sewing the binding to the quilt.

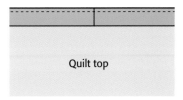

Diagonal Connections

When joining the ends of the binding, use a diagonal connection to distribute the layers of fabric.

Folded Connection

1. Approximately 4" from your starting point, stop sewing the binding to the quilt. Leaving a 2" overlap with the beginning of the binding, unfold the end and trim it diagonally so that when refolded, the shorter end will be on top as shown.

2. Turn the diagonal edge under ¼", and insert the beginning "tail" into the diagonal fold.

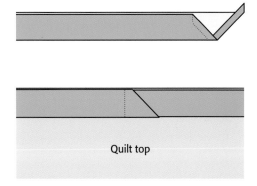

3. Continue sewing the binding to the quilt. You can leave this diagonal seam unstitched, but it is more commonly hand stitched closed after the binding has been stitched to the back of the quilt.

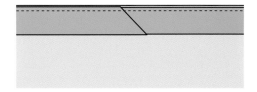

Diagonal Seam

1. Stop sewing the binding approximately 6" away from the starting point. Cut the end of your binding with a perpendicular cut so that it overlaps the beginning end of your binding. The length of the overlap must equal the width of your binding strip. (For example, use a 2" overlap for 2"-wide binding and a 2½" overlap for 2½"-wide binding.)

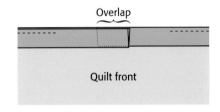

2. Open the folds of the two strips and overlap them at right angles with right sides together as shown. Pin them together. Draw a diagonal line between the two points where the binding strips intersect as shown. (Remember the *A* on page 35?)

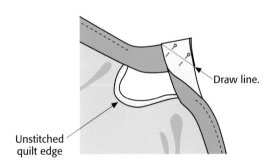

3. Sew the ends together on the marked line and then trim the seam allowance to ¼". Press the seam allowance open.

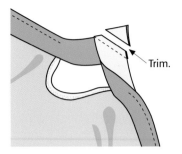

4. Refold the seamed section of the strip, return it to the edge of the quilt, and finish sewing the binding in place. A perfect fit!

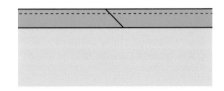

Binding Special Edges

Sometimes quilts don't have four straight sides and square corners. With a little extra effort, you can bind quilts with any of the special edge treatments to perfection.

Scalloped Edges

Scalloped edges create a beautiful finish, especially on romantic appliqué quilts. Scallops allow quilters to reflect elements of the interior quilt design in the border, as in Double Wedding Ring or Dresden Plate patterns. Binding for scalloped edges—or any type of curve—should always be cut on the true bias so that it will flex smoothly around the curves while remaining flat. You can use either single- or double-fold binding.

Sewing binding on scalloped edges is a combination of two processes: applying the binding around a curve and turning an inside corner. If you have ever rounded off the corners of a quilt to apply binding, you are halfway there!

1. Carefully baste the three quilt layers together ⅛" inside the cut scalloped edges. Basting is especially important because the bias curves can stretch under the presser foot as you sew on the machine. If your scallops are simply marked on straight borders but have not been cut, you can apply the binding to the marked fabric and trim excess fabric from the curves later.

2. Apply the binding, starting along one side of a curve. Starting on the outer edge of the curve may be noticeable when you finish. Starting at the inside corner may cause problems when you are ending your binding.

   Be careful not to stretch the binding as you place it around the curve. Position the binding so that the cut edge of the binding matches the cut edge of the curve. As you pin the binding around the curve, ease the fullness in the binding so that it matches the seam line of the quilt. You can pin the binding around one curve at a time before you sew.

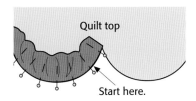

Quilt top

Start here.

3. As you sew around the curve, use a long straight pin to help you guide the fabric under the presser foot on your sewing machine. Easing the fullness of the binding around the curves allows the binding to turn over the curve of the scallop and lie flat when it is finished. Stop sewing when you reach the inside corner. Mark the inside corner point with a pin so that you'll know where to stop.

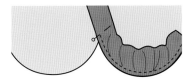

4. Leave the needle in the fabric and lift the presser foot. Turn the binding so that it's ready to stitch onto the next scallop. Pivot the quilt, lower the presser foot, and stitch for about 1" along the next scallop. While the quilt is still under the needle, pin the binding to the next scallop and proceed.

5. Finish the bias binding with a diagonal join as described on page 34.

6. Turn the binding to the back of the quilt one scallop at a time. When you reach an inside corner, turn one side of the corner to the back and pin it. As you turn the second side of the corner, a tuck will form a folded miter. The deepest part of the tuck will be at the outer edge of the binding. As the binding turns to the back of the quilt, the fold will taper to lie flat along the sewing line. Stitch the folded miter closed with a blind stitch.

Quilt back

Sculpted Edges

Sculpted edges feature curves that flow around the edge of the quilt. The design can include outside points, which are treated like corners, or inside points, which are handled like scallops. Because some of the edges are curved, you should cut the binding on the bias so that it will be easy to maneuver smoothly around the curves.

- As you apply the binding to outside or convex curves, ease the binding around the curve as for scalloped edges (see page 53).

- As you apply the binding to inside or concave curves, stretch the binding just slightly so that it will lie flat and not pucker on the edges once it is turned over the quilt edge.

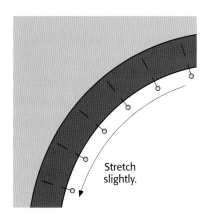

Stretch slightly.

- On outside points, follow the directions for "Folded Mitered Corners" on page 46.

- On inside points, follow the directions for inside points found in "Scalloped Edges."

Grandmother's Flower Garden Edges

The edges on Grandmother's Flower Garden quilts are a series of 60° angles. The easiest way to bind these edges is to use 1"-wide single-fold binding cut on the bias and ¼"-wide seam allowances. This will make it easier to ease and stretch around all the patchwork angles. As you approach an outside angle, instead of folding miters, ease the binding to go around the point. On the inside angles, stretch the binding slightly so that it will lie flat on the edge of the quilt. Turn the binding over the edge for a ¼" finish.

*I*f you are a creative quilter, try a special finishing technique for the edge of your quilt. Insert covered cording in the binding or between the front and back of the quilt for a coordinating accent or to complement one of the colors in your quilt. A fun finish for a scrappy quilt is to add prairie points. You'll need extra fabric to make the points, but they create a unique border for your design. A baby quilt or a feminine design may lend itself to a ruffled edge. Ruffles require extra fabric, so plan ahead. You can repeat a favorite fabric in the ruffle or use pregathered eyelet lace or gathered trim for a fun and frivolous edge.

Attaching Special Finishes

You can add a special touch by sewing covered cording, flat lace, piping, or rickrack into your binding. After completing the quilting on your project, prepare the edges for binding. Stitch the trim around the edges of your quilt, and then apply the binding over the trim to cover the raw edges.

If you want to insert covered cording, prairie points, gathered lace, or ruffles between the front and back of your quilt without also adding binding, simply stitch the trim to the quilt top and use the backing to finish the edges. It's easiest to sew the trim to the quilt top before quilting your project, but if you decide to add trim after the quilting has been completed, you can still do so. Just make sure that no quilting stitches lie within ½" of the quilt edges so that you can sew the trim to the front and then turn under the seam allowance.

Method 1: Attaching Trim before Quilting

1. Sew the desired trim around the front edge of the quilt top, using a ¼" seam allowance.

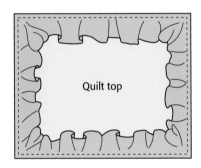

2. Place the front and back of the quilt right sides together, sandwiching the trim inside, and pin around the edges. With the quilt top on top, sew around the quilt edges just inside the previous ¼" seam. Leave a 10" opening to turn the quilt right side out. Backstitch along each side of the opening.

3. Attach the batting, referring to the machine-finishing directions in "Finishing Edges without Binding" on page 20 to complete your quilt.

4. Turn the quilt right side out and stitch the opening closed with a slip stitch.

Method 2: Attaching Trim after Quilting

Make sure that your quilting stitches stop at least ½" from the edge of the quilt top to allow room for sewing the trim to the front and turning under the seam allowance.

1. Sew the trim to the front edge of the quilt and the batting only. Fold the backing out of the way as you sew. Attach the prairie points, lace, ruffles, or cording to the right side of the quilt top, using a ¼" seam allowance and sewing through the quilt top and batting.

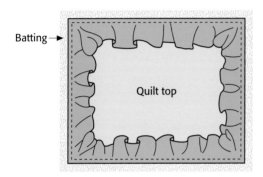

2. Trim the batting close to the stitching.

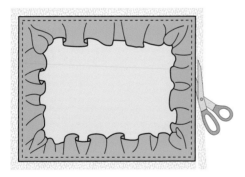

3. Fold the trim out, away from the quilt, turning the seam allowance in, toward the batting. Press lightly on the right side.

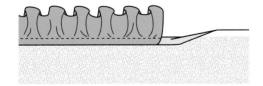

4. Turn the seam allowance of the backing fabric under ¼" and pin the back of the quilt to the back side of the trim, covering the seam allowance and the machine stitches. Complete the back of the quilt using a blind stitch or slip stitch.

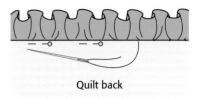

Quilt back

Adding Covered Cording

Covered cording creates a thin line of trim that can be used along the edge of your quilt with or without adding binding. When used with binding, it shows up as a spark of color between the quilt top and the binding. When used without binding, it is inserted between the front and back of the quilt to accent a color or fabric in the quilt and give the illusion of very thin binding.

Uncovered cotton cording is available in most fabric stores. Purchase enough to go the distance around the quilt, plus ¼ yard. Choose 1/16"- to ¼"-diameter cording, depending on the look you desire. To cover the cording, cut 1"-wide fabric strips and piece them together to equal the length of your cording. You can use either bias or straight-grain strips. If you'll be applying the covered cording to curves, the fabric strips should be cut on the bias.

1. To cover the cording, fold the fabric strip in half lengthwise, wrong sides together. Insert the cording, pushing it snugly against the fold.

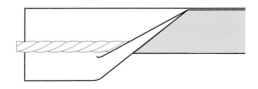

2. Use a zipper foot on your sewing machine and set the needle so that it sews to the left of the foot. Sew the two cut edges of the fabric together using a long (basting) stitch, enclosing the cording. The zipper foot should ride comfortably along the right side of the cording.

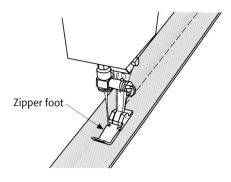

Zipper foot

3. When you've enclosed the entire piece of cording, trim the seam allowance evenly to ¼".

Attaching Covered Cording with Binding

Add a tailored effect to a quilt by sewing a row of covered cording inside the binding edge. This technique adds thickness to the edge of the quilt. When planning, you should add ¼" to the cut width of your binding so that it will turn over the edge. You can trim the edge of the quilt slightly after you apply the binding if it will not fully cover the stitches on the back of the quilt.

1. Make covered cording, following the preceding directions and using your desired fabric. The cording should be thin, approximately ¹⁄₁₆" to ⅛" in diameter, so that it adds just a slim accent to the edge of your quilt.

Covered cording   Binding

Quilt top

2. Baste the quilt layers together (see page 41). Sew the cording to the edge of the quilt, using your zipper foot and a long basting stitch. Use the seam allowance you plan for your binding.

3. If you are sewing covered cording around a curve, avoid stretching it as you sew. The cording does not have to be eased like binding; just sew it evenly to the edge of the quilt. Clip the cording seam allowance a few times to keep it flat. Do not clip any further than the stitching line.

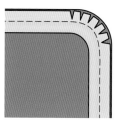

Finishing Edges with Special Techniques

4. When you approach a corner, stop sewing 1" from the corner. Clip the covered cording seam allowance three or four times near the corner. Continue stitching to the corner. Stop with the needle in the fabric and lift the presser foot. Turn the fabric slightly and take two stitches. Lift the presser foot again and turn the fabric to sew the next side. These two stitches will help the corner look sharp.

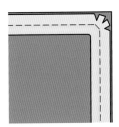

5. To end the cording, see step 3, below right. Then apply the binding on top of the cording, using your zipper foot.

6. As you turn the binding to the back of the quilt, the cording will appear between the quilt and the binding. Before you sew the binding on the back of the quilt, inspect your cording carefully. You might need to resew the binding in a few spots to cover the cording stitches.

Attaching Covered Cording without Binding

Because no binding will be attached in this method, the covered cording will stand alone as a narrow finish on the edge of your quilt.

1. Place the covered cording along the edge of the quilt top, matching the cut edge of the cording with the cut edge of the quilt. Using a zipper foot, sew the cording to the quilt top (not to the batting or backing) using a ¼" seam allowance.

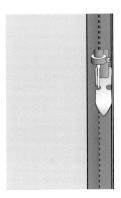

2. If you need to sew around a curve or corner, refer to step 4, above left.
3. When you approach the starting point, cut the covered cording so that the two tails overlap 1". Open the stitches on one tail and cut off 1" of just the cording, not the fabric covering. Turn the cut edge of this fabric covering under ¼", either straight or diagonally. Insert the beginning tail, refold the fabric to cover all raw edges, and continue the seam.

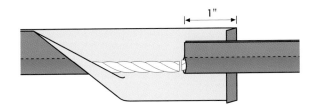

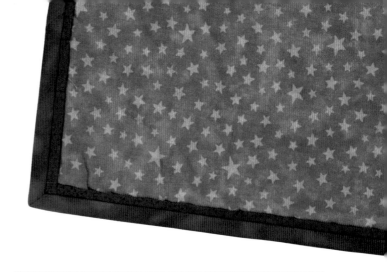

4. Sew the front and back of the quilt together by machine, referring to "Attaching Special Finishes" on page 55. Continue to use a zipper foot, which will ride easily next to the cording thickness and position your stitches correctly. If you sew with the front of the quilt on top, you will be able to see your previous stitches. Sew to the left of these stitches to hide them in the seam of the finished quilt.

Adding Flat Piping

Flat piping is also used to add a hint of an accent color to the edge of the quilt between the quilt top and the binding.

1. Cut enough 1"-wide strips of accent fabric to go around the outside of the quilt. Piece them together using a diagonal seam (see page 35) so that you have one strip for each side of the quilt.

2. Fold the strips in half lengthwise, wrong sides together, and position them so that the raw edges are aligned with the quilt edges. Baste the strips to the quilt edges using a scant ¼" seam allowance. Overlap the strips in the corners.

3. Apply the binding on top of the piping.

4. When you turn the binding to the back of the quilt, the piping will appear between the quilt and the binding. Finish the binding by hand, stitching the folded edge to the back of the quilt.

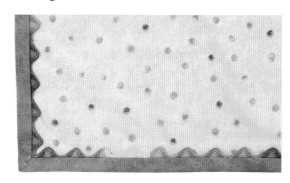

Happy Ending Hint

You can add other interesting edge treatments just as you would add the flat piping:

Lace: Follow the directions for "Flat Piping" to insert narrow, flat lace inside the binding for a feminine touch to your quilt.

Rickrack: Sew rickrack along the edge of your quilt before attaching the binding. As you turn the binding to the back of the quilt, the rickrack will appear between the quilt and the binding for a fun finish.

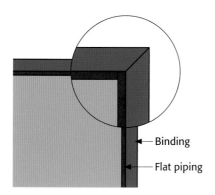

Individual Prairie Points

1. To make one prairie point, cut a 3" square of fabric. Fold the square in half diagonally, wrong sides together. Fold the square diagonally again, forming a smaller triangle. Once folded, the longest edge of the triangle will be attached to the edge of the quilt. After accounting for the seam allowance, the finished prairie point will be approximately 2½" wide at the base and 1¼" tall. If you want larger prairie points, you can start with 3½" or 4" squares.

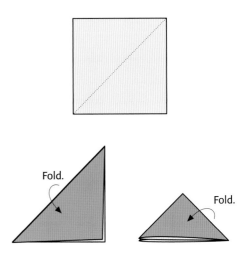

Fold.   Fold.

2. Make another prairie point, and then slip the fold of one point into the opening of the first one. This is how they fit together to go around your quilt. They can overlap a little or a lot, depending on the look you want or on the amount of fabric you have available.

3. For a large quilt, make a long string of points before sewing them to the quilt edge. Start feeding the first point into your sewing machine, placing the cut edges on the right as you sew, and the folded tip under the needle. Sew for 1", using a basting stitch, and then feed the next point into

Adding Prairie Points

Prairie points are small folded triangles placed along the edge of the quilt. They can repeat a triangular motif in the design of your quilt, duplicate the color scheme of the quilt, or accent the design. Prairie points can be all the same color, or they can repeat a variety of fabrics in the quilt. If you want your prairie points to be assorted, you'll need to make individual prairie points. If your plan is for all of them to be the same fabric, then you can use the continuous prairie-point method on page 63.

If you start with 3" squares (as described in our example at right), every 20" of quilt edge takes approximately 12 prairie points when they are overlapped. If the points are placed side by side along the edge seam, each point takes 2½". One yard of fabric is enough to make prairie points for a 60" square quilt. A full- or queen-size quilt requires 1½ yards, and a king-size quilt requires 2 yards.

the first one, overlapping them by approximately ¾". Continue sewing and feeding prairie points until you have enough length for the edges of your quilt. Make a separate string of points for each side of your quilt.

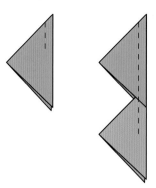

4. If your quilt is small or if you want to be more accurate about the placement of the points, you can position the points on the edge of the quilt before you sew them together. Start by placing one point in the center of one side of your quilt, with the long cut edge of the triangle matching the cut edge of the front of your quilt.

   Place a prairie point at each end of the quilt side, making sure that the folded edges of the triangles aim in the same direction as the first one. Place another prairie point between these triangles, and then continue to arrange more folded triangles in between until the side of the quilt is full. You can overlap them a little or a lot, as long as they are evenly spaced.

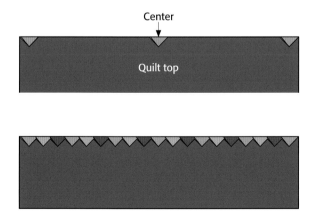

5. In the corners of the quilt, place two prairie points as shown so that they fit together side by side. They should not overlap. When you sew them onto the quilt edge, pivot your seam where they meet. When they are turned to point out, there will be a perfect corner.

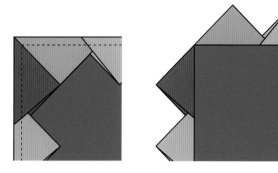

6. To sew the prairie points onto your quilt, first pin the cut edge of the points to the cut edge of the quilt top. If you have made a long string of points, make sure that you have the same number of points on opposite sides of your quilt. You may need to shift a few of the prairie points near the quilt ends as you go to fit the side of the quilt accurately. Sew the prairie points to all four edges of your quilt, using a ¼" seam. To finish sewing your quilt together, refer to "Attaching Special Finishes" on page 55.

Happy Ending Hint

For a different effect, you can fold fabric squares in half horizontally instead of diagonally. Then fold the two ends in toward the center on the diagonal as shown. This method gives a symmetrical appearance to the folded triangles. When they are applied to your quilt, these triangles look nice if they are stitched side by side rather than overlapped along the edge.

For an extra special look, make the prairie points from pieced squares. When they are folded, the accent color will appear inside each triangle. You can use either the diagonal or horizontal folding method as shown.

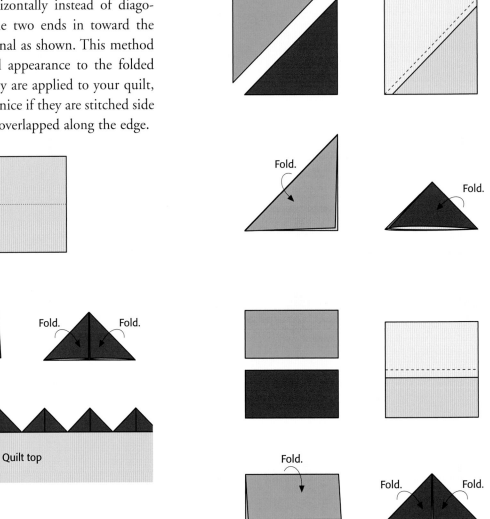

Continuous Prairie Points

A quick way to add prairie points is to make a continuous strip of them that fits the edge of your quilt. To fit the edges of the quilt accurately, you must be able to divide the side of your quilt equally by the size of the prairie points. In the following step-by-step instructions, we'll use 3" prairie points as an example, but you can adjust the size of the cut prairie points to 2½" or 3½" if that works better for your quilt size.

1. Cut strips twice as wide as the finished measurement of the prairie point. For 3" points, you'd cut 6"-wide strips.

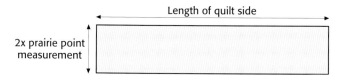

2. To determine the length of the strips, measure the edges of your quilt. For a small quilt, cut individual strips of fabric the length of each side. For a large quilt, cut multiple strips that add up to the total length of the quilt, keeping in mind that you'll overlap the individual strips later on as you pin them to the quilt edge.

Happy Endings Hint

If the edge of your quilt can't be divided equally by the size of the prairie points, you may be able to trim the border of your quilt slightly to accommodate the prairie points. On a large quilt, you can adjust segments as you overlap them to fit the length of each quilt side.

3. Press the strip in half lengthwise, wrong sides together, to mark the vertical center. Unfold the strip and, on one side of the fold, draw lines dividing the strip into 3"-square segments. On the other side of the fold line, first mark a 1½"-wide segment (half of the 3" measurement), and then mark 3"-square segments until you have another 1½" segment remaining at the end.

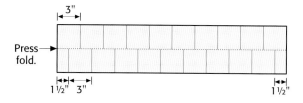

4. Using scissors, cut on the marked side lines. Cut off the 1½" segments. Do not cut through the center fold line.

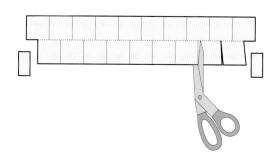

5. Working on an ironing board, start on one side of the strip and fold the first square in half diagonally, and then in half again, as shown, to form a prairie point. Press each square as you fold it.

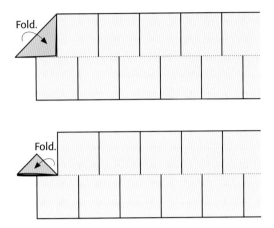

6. Move to the other side of the center line and fold the next square once diagonally, starting with the edge near the last prairie point.

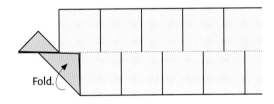

7. Flip the first prairie point over the folded square. Press the second diagonal fold in the second prairie point, overlapping the first one. Place a pin at the bottom edge of the point to hold it in place.

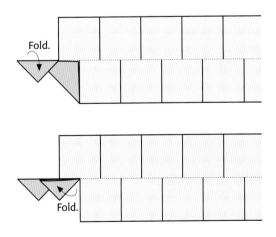

8. Continue folding and nesting the squares on the strip until the entire strip is folded. Machine baste ⅛" from the edge of the strip to secure the points.

9. Attach the strips of prairie points to the edges of the quilt, aligning the straight edge of the prairie points with the raw edge of the quilt and overlapping segments as needed. Make sure that the prairie points meet at the corners (see page 61). To attach the strips, sew around all four edges of the quilt front using a ¼" seam allowance. To finish sewing your quilt together, refer to "Attaching Special Finishes" on page 55.

Adding Gathered Lace or Ruffles

For a feminine touch, you can add gathered lace or ruffles to the edge of a quilt. Look for lace that is pregathered rather than flat. Sometimes you can find premade fabric ruffles, too. But more than likely, you'll need to make your own ruffles if that's the look you want. Besides, that way, you can match the ruffles perfectly to your quilt fabrics. When you purchase pregathered trim, use the distance around the quilt, plus ¼ yard. If you plan to make your own ruffles, see "Making Your Own Ruffles" on page 66.

1. Place the ruffles or gathered-lace trim, right sides together, on the quilt top, matching the cut edge of the quilt and the raw edge or binding edge of the trim.

2. Using a ¼" seam allowance, sew just to the left of the gathering line or bound edge of the trim so that any gathering stitches will be captured in the seam allowance and won't show on the finished quilt. Leave the first 2" of trim free so that you'll have a "tail" for finishing later.

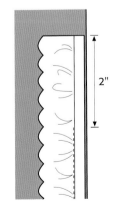

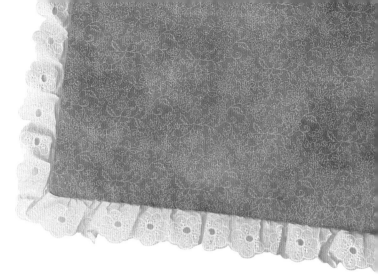

3. Sew along the first edge of the quilt, stopping 1" from the corner. For this last inch, as you approach the square corner, use a long straight pin to push the ruffle or lace under the presser foot, adding more fullness to the gathers.

When you get to the corner, leave the needle in the fabric, lift the presser foot, and pivot to stitch the next side. Continue adding fullness to the gathers for another inch. This will give your ruffle enough fullness to "fan out" around the corner when it is turned right side out. Even if your corners are rounded off, it is still helpful to add some fullness as you sew the ruffle or lace around the curve.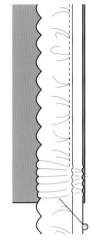

4. After you've stitched around the entire quilt and are approaching the starting point, you have a few options for finishing the ruffle or lace. To make a seam in the ruffle, cut the two ends so that they overlap ½". Place the two ends right sides together and sew a ¼" seam. Press the seam to one side and then finish sewing the ruffle or lace to the quilt.

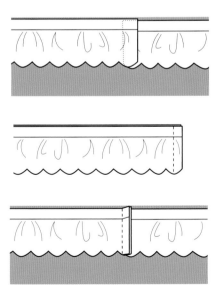

5. For a quicker finish, you can fold the beginning tail back 1". Cut the ending tail so that it overlaps the first one by 1". Sew over these folds, and the completed ruffle or lace will show no raw edges on the right side. The fullness of the ruffles will hide the cut edges.

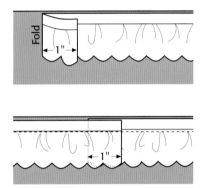

6. If your pregathered ruffle is doubled, you can conceal the cut edges by trimming the tails so that they overlap 2". Fold the raw edges of one tail ½" to the inside and then slip the other tail inside the fold, too. This will provide a finished edge on the front and the back.

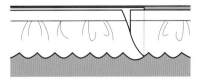

7. To finish sewing your quilt together, refer "Attaching Special Finishes" on page 55.

seam. When all strips are sewn together, join the two ends to make a continuous loop.

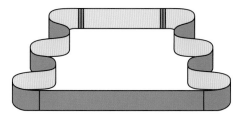

Making Your Own Ruffles

For a perfect match, make your own ruffles to coordinate with the fabrics and colors in your quilt. Fabric ruffles can be cut on the bias or straight grain of the fabric. Cut the fabric strips twice the width of the finished ruffle, plus two seam allowances. For example, if you want a 2"-wide finished ruffle, cut 4½"-wide strips (2" for the front, 2" for the back, and two ¼" seam allowances). By making a doubled ruffle, it will be just as pretty on the back of the quilt as it is on the front. Plus, you won't have to sew a long hem on the outer edge of the ruffle.

You'll need enough fabric strips to make a continuous strip that is at least twice the distance around your quilt. As an example, a 36"-square baby quilt measures 4 yards around the perimeter. To make a nice, full ruffle for that quilt, you need to cut 8 yards of fabric strips. That's not 8 yards of fabric, but strips that will be 8 yards long when sewn together end to end.

1. Stitch the fabric strips together to make one long strip. Unlike joining binding strips, it's best to sew a perpendicular seam across the end of the strips, as shown, rather than diagonally. With right sides together, sew the strips using ¼" seams. Press the seams open to distribute the thickness of the

2. Fold the ruffle in half, wrong sides together, so that the cut edges are aligned. Press the fold with a steam iron to help the layers stay together.

3. Fold the length, to divide it in half, and mark these points with pins. Fold each section in half again to divide the strip into quarters, and mark these points with pins. These marks will be used to position the ruffle evenly on the quilt.

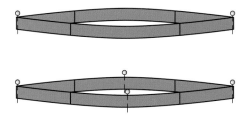

4. To gather the ruffle, sew two parallel lines of machine basting stitches ⅛" and ⅜" from the cut edges of the ruffle. Gather the ruffle by pulling the bobbin threads—and praying that they don't break! Gather each quarter of the ruffle separately to prevent breaking the threads. (See the accompanying "Happy Ending Hint," opposite.)

Happy Ending Hint

Here's a great way to gather ruffles—and you don't have to worry about your bobbin thread breaking. It's especially helpful for yards of ruffles, where the chance of breaking a thread is pretty high.

Set your sewing machine for the longest, widest zigzag stitch it will make. Lay a piece of pearl cotton, crochet cotton, or even dental floss ⅛" from the cut edges of the ruffle. Zigzag over this thread, being careful not to stitch into it. When you are finished, this thread can be pulled easily to gather the ruffle. Just be sure to anchor one end of the thread so that you don't accidentally pull it out from under the zigzag stitches.

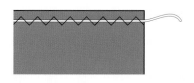

5. Gather the ruffle to fit the edge of your quilt. The four pins placed along the ruffle can be matched to the centers of the quilt sides. For a large quilt, you can divide the ruffle length again to make it easier to handle. Distribute the fullness evenly along the edge, but add extra gathers for 1" on each side of the corners to allow the ruffle to lie flat when it is turned out (see page 65, step 3).

6. Sew the ruffle to the edges of the quilt top with a ¼" seam allowance. To finish sewing your quilt together, refer to "Attaching Special Finishes" on page 55.

Final Touches

Ah, your project is quilted and the edges are bound—it's finished! But before you turn off the machine and close the sewing room door behind you, there are a couple of things you may want to add to your special quilt.

Quilt Labels

You've finished your quilt by sewing the last 3" of binding securely, and you can't wait to take it upstairs and fling it on the bed to admire its total beauty!

But wait! Take a few moments to share some information with future generations. Sign your newest "work of heart" with your name and other information you would like to remember. Record the date, celebrate the occasion, and dedicate it to someone special. Your quilt is now a part of history, and you want to remember its story. Don't you wish your grandmother had done this with her quilts?

You can sign your quilt several ways. You can embroider or quilt an inscription on the front of your quilt. You can use a fine-line permanent marker to write the information in a corner on the back of the quilt. Or you can make a "designer" label to sew to the back of your quilt.

- Iron a piece of freezer paper to the wrong side of your label fabric. The freezer paper will stabilize the fabric and keep it from stretching as you write. Using a fine-line permanent marker, write your information and sign your name for a personalized quilt label.

- Type the information you want, using a pretty font on your computer. Print it on paper and then use a light box to trace the information onto your fabric label with a permanent marker.

- It's possible to print your label right onto fabric. Iron freezer paper to your label fabric and cut it to measure exactly 8½" x 11". Send this piece through your printer to make a quick label. Test the label to see if it's colorfast. You may need to purchase a product at your local quilt shop that keeps the ink from smudging or running.

- Chart your information on graph paper and embroider a label in counted cross-stitch.

The information you put on your quilt label will help to bring back special memories. (And after you have finished 10 more quilts, you'll see why it's a good thing you recorded the information when you did!) Your family and friends will cherish your special "signed" gifts. It will help historians of the future remember you and help ensure a happy ending for your quilt.

Hanging Sleeves

If you are planning to hang your quilt on a wall (or in a quilt show), sew a sleeve to the back. You can either do this before applying the binding or after. The sleeve should be made from a tube of fabric. When you slide the hanging rod into the sleeve, the back of the quilt will be protected.

Some quilters sew a second hanging sleeve to the bottom of the quilt. A dowel placed in this sleeve will add weight to the quilt and help it hang straight.

If your quilt is very wide, it's a good idea to sew two smaller hanging sleeves with a space in the middle, rather than one long sleeve all the way across the back of the quilt. That way, when you hang the quilt, you can use a nail or hook to support the center of the dowel and the quilt so that the quilt won't sag.

If you haven't attached the binding yet, use the procedure immediately following. If you have already attached the binding, see the alternate method for attaching a sleeve, opposite.

Method One

1. Cut a strip of fabric as long as the width of your quilt and 8½" wide. This strip will make a 4"-wide sleeve. To create a deeper sleeve, double the desired finished width and add ½" for seam allowances. If, for example, you wish to add a 6"-wide sleeve, cut the sleeve 12½" wide. If you're planning to enter your quilt in a show, check the specifications before attaching a sleeve. A 4"-wide sleeve is commonly called for, but standards may differ from one quilt show to another.

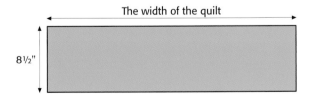

The width of the quilt

8½"

2. Turn under ¼" twice at each short end of the strip and stitch a narrow hem.

3. Fold the sleeve lengthwise, wrong sides together, and pin the raw edges to the top of the quilt before you attach the binding. Machine baste ⅛" from the top edge.

Fold

Quilt back

4. Sew the binding to the quilt. The raw edges of the sleeve will be covered when the binding is turned to the back of the quilt.

5. Pin the folded edge of the sleeve to the back of the quilt. Blindstitch the sleeve to the back of the quilt, being very careful not to stitch through to the front of the quilt.

Happy Ending Hint

When you pin the bottom of the sleeve to the back of the quilt, roll the edge up ¼". This adds a little extra room for the hanging rod and will help the front of the quilt hang smoothly.

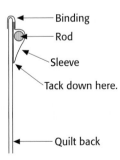

Binding
Rod
Sleeve
Tack down here.
Quilt back

Method Two

If you already stitched the binding on your quilt, you can still sew a hanging sleeve to the back.

1. Follow steps 1 and 2 on page 69 to prepare the strip for the sleeve.
2. Fold the sleeve, wrong sides together, match the long sides, and sew a ¼" seam.

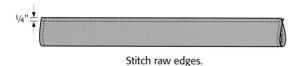

Stitch raw edges.

3. Arrange the seam in the center of the strip and press the seam open to distribute the thickness of the seam allowance.

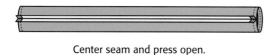

Center seam and press open.

4. Place the hanging sleeve on the back of the quilt, just under the binding at the top of the quilt. The seam allowance will be hidden against the back of the quilt.

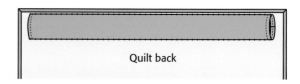

Quilt back

5. Slip-stitch the edges of the hanging sleeve to the back of the quilt.

I've included a guide to hand and machine stitches that will help you find the appropriate stitches for your project.

Hand Stitches

You can use hand stitches to sew patchwork or appliqué designs, to stitch the front and back of the quilt together, to connect binding strips, to make covered cording, or to sew the binding to your quilt. Use a secure running stitch to sew the layers of fabric together.

1. Cut a single strand of thread about 18" long and tie a knot in one end.
2. Using a Sharp or milliner's needle, or a Between if you prefer a shorter needle, take two or three short running stitches at a time, sewing in and out through the layers of fabric to hold them together. Make a small backstitch every 2" to strengthen the running stitches. End your stitches by sewing two small backstitches, bringing the needle through the loop to secure your thread.

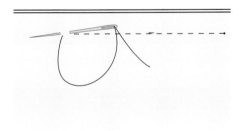

Quilting Stitches

Quilting stitches are short running stitches used to sew the front, batting, and back of your quilt together.

1. Thread a Between quilting needle with an 18" length of hand-quilting thread and tie a single knot in the long end of the thread. Insert the needle through the top layer of the quilt about ¾" away from the point where you want to start stitching. Slide the needle through the batting layer and bring the needle out at the starting point.
2. Gently tug on the thread until the knot pops through the fabric and is buried in the batting. Take a backstitch and begin quilting, making a small running stitch that goes through all three layers. Take two, three, or four stitches at a time, trying to keep them straight and even.
3. To end a line of quilting, make a single knot approximately ¼" from your quilt top. Take one more backstitch into your quilt, tugging the knot into the batting layer and bringing the needle out ¾" away from your stitches. Clip the thread and let the end disappear into your quilt.

Hand Quilting Stitch

Basting Stitches

Basting stitches are used to hold layers of fabric together while you sew the final seam. They are usually removed after the seam has been sewn. Basting stitches are long running stitches, stitched with the "ins" and "outs" approximately 1" apart. They are usually stitched one or two stitches at a time. You do not need to make knots or backstitches because you want these stitches to be easy to remove later.

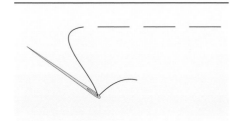

Finishing Stitches

Use the blind stitch—sometimes called the appliqué stitch—and the slip stitch—sometimes called the ladder stitch—to finish the front and back of the quilt without binding, after turning the back of the quilt to finish the front of the quilt, or after applying binding or special finishings. These stitches are invisible when your quilt is finished.

Use the following suggestions regarding needles and threads for a perfect finish to your edge treatment:

- Use a Sharp or milliner's needle, or use a Between if you prefer a shorter needle.

- Start with a single strand of thread approximately 18" long and tie a knot in the long end.

- Use a single thread; double thread tends to twist and weaken the stitches.

- Match the thread to the binding if your binding is a different color than your quilt.

- Match the thread to the front of the quilt when sewing the front and back together.

- Match the thread to the back of the quilt when finishing prairie points, ruffles, lace, and cording.

Blind Stitch or Appliqué Stitch

A blind stitch is appropriate to use on all areas of the binding. It is used when you make your own binding or when you use the quilt backing to finish the edges. This stitch can also be used to sew the back of the quilt to prairie points, ruffles, lace, or cording. The blind stitch is a good stitch to use on details such as folded mitered corners or at the end of the binding. It is traditionally used to sew appliqués to background fabric.

Mimi's Favorite

I love the blind stitch! It's really the traditional appliqué stitch. I love to finish the binding cuddled up with the quilt in my favorite chair, with my favorite bright light and a cup of tea.

1. Bring your needle up through the edge of the binding, as close as possible to the folded edge.

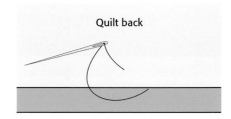

Quilt back

2. Make a very small stitch by moving the needle straight off the edge of the binding and into the quilt. This stitch should be taken just past the machine stitches that were used to apply the binding to the quilt. When the binding is finished, these machine stitches will be covered.

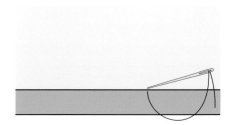

3. Slide your needle under the top layer of the quilt, guiding it through the batting for approximately ⅛" to ¼". These stitches should not go all the way through to the other side of the quilt. Bring the needle back up through the quilt and the folded edge of the binding, picking up only one or two threads from the fold.

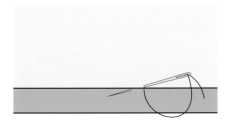

4. Continue this process, pulling the thread slightly after every four or five stitches. The stitches should disappear into the seam.

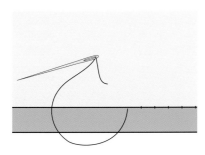

5. When you get to a folded mitered corner, you may want to secure the miter by stitching the folds closed. Pin the miter folds so that they are neat, using the needle or a long straight pin to tuck the folds in place evenly. Stitch the miter on the back side of the quilt, using four or five blind stitches.

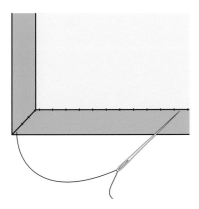

Happy Ending Hint

As you finish your quilt, don't pin the binding around the entire quilt. All you need is four or five straight pins or binding clips. Pin or clip just a few inches at a time as you sew by hand. Before long, those pins will travel around the whole quilt. As a bonus, the quilt will not stick you if you curl up in it to complete your last stitches.

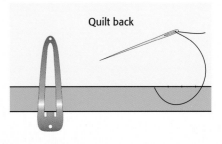

6. At the outer point, move the needle through to the front of the miter and stitch the miter on the front of the quilt, continuing to the inner miter corner.

7. Check to see if there is a space between the rows of machine stitches in the corner. One or two small stitches can close this space easily.

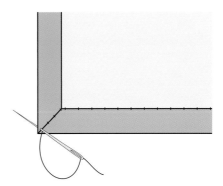

8. Now stick the needle through to the back side of the quilt and continue to attach the binding on the back side. This same process can be used to close the fold where you begin and end your binding.

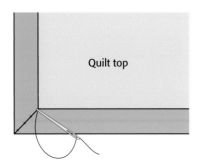

Quilt top

Slip Stitch or Ladder Stitch

A slip stitch is used to finish the front and back without binding, to sew the straight edges of the binding, and to attach the back of the quilt to prairie points, ruffles, pleats, or cording. It is a good stitch to use on long, straight areas.

1. Bring your needle up through the folded edge of the binding. Take a small stitch in the fold of the binding, approximately ⅛" to ¼" long.

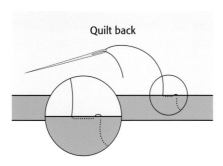

Quilt back

2. Move straight across to the quilt and take a small stitch in the top layer of the quilt, just past the machine stitches that were used to apply the binding.

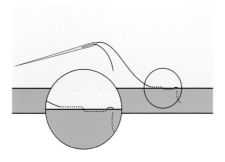

3. Now move your needle straight across to the binding and take a small stitch in the fold. Repeat until you have five or six stitches between the quilt and the binding. The stitches will resemble the rungs on a ladder.

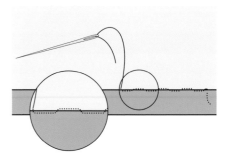

4. Pull lightly on the thread until the stitches disappear. Take care not to pull too tightly or the fabric will pucker.

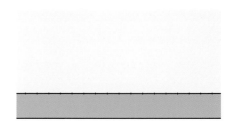

Ending Stitches

When you start to run out of thread, it's time to end your stitches.

1. Lift up the binding and take a small stitch in the seam allowance. Take two backstitches to tie a knot in the thread, stitching through the loops as you take the stitches. These stitches will be under the binding when you continue and will never be seen.

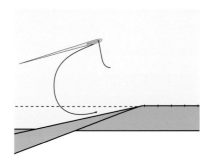

2. When you get to the end of the binding, take two small backstitches near the last stitch, slide the needle through the top layer of the quilt about an inch, and bring the thread out. Clip the thread and you are done!

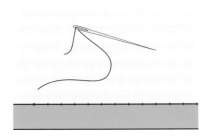

Machine Stitches

When you are constructing your quilt, sewing the front and back together, or applying binding or special finishings, set the stitch length on your machine to 10 to 12 stitches per inch. This stitch length is very secure, but it's also just the right size for your seam ripper (just in case you need to use it).

Machine Piecing

When sewing binding strips together to make a long strip, or making continuous binding, set the stitch length on your machine to a shorter 12 to 15 stitches per inch. These small stitches will hold the pieces together without backstitching, especially as you cut continuous binding strips apart.

Machine Basting

Use a machine basting stitch with a length of six stitches per inch when you are basting quilt layers together, preparing a string of prairie points, gathering ruffles, or making covered cording. These longer stitches hold fabric together but are easy to remove if necessary.

Machine-Finished Binding

It's possible to apply the binding on your quilt entirely by using the sewing machine.

1. To apply single-fold or double-fold binding, sew the binding to the back of the quilt rather than to the front. When the binding is turned to the front of the quilt, the finishing machine stitches will be on the front.

2. Turn the binding to the front of the quilt. Carefully pin all around the quilt to keep the binding in place and prevent it from slipping. Pin the mitered corners securely. Make sure that the binding covers the machine stitches that were used to sew the binding to the quilt.

3. Machine stitch the binding to the quilt along the fold at the inner edge of the binding. You will be sewing through the binding fold, the three layers of the quilt, and the binding on the back of the quilt. This may be very bulky, but it can be controlled. You may need to use a long straight pin to adjust the fold as it goes under the machine presser foot. The machine stitches produce a nice edge to the binding on the front of the quilt, but it's difficult to control the position of the stitches on the back of the quilt. This may not be the method to use on your heirloom or prizewinning quilt, but it is a quick way to finish the binding.

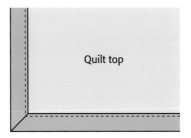

Quilt top

4. If your quilt has mitered corners, it is best to ignore the miters as you sew around the binding by machine. Turn the corner when you get to the inside miter corner and continue stitching. The miter will survive if you just leave it folded, but you can close the miter using hand blind stitches.

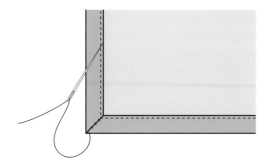

5. As you stitch around the quilt, continue sewing over the point where the binding starts and ends.

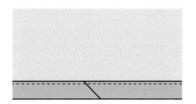

6. As you finish sewing the binding with your sewing machine, overlap your beginning stitches for 2" and backstitch.

7. An invisible machine blind stitch can be used to finish your binding. Set the stitch so that the straight stitches are placed on the quilt top and the zigzag stitches just catch the edge of the binding.

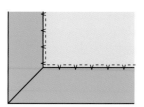

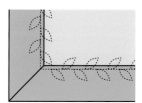

8. Use decorative machine stitches to add a special finish to your binding if desired.

Index

*M*imi Dietrich has been sewing since she was a young teenager and quilting since 1974. She lives in Baltimore, Maryland, with her husband, Bob. Her sons are grown and life is good! She loves appliqué—especially the album quilts that are so famous in her hometown. Mimi has written 10 books for That Patchwork Place. Happy Endings was her first book, originally published 15 years ago.

new and bestselling titles from

America's Best-Loved Craft & Hobby Books®

America's Best-Loved Quilt Books®

NEW RELEASES
1000 Great Quilt Blocks
Basically Brilliant Knits
Bright Quilts from Down Under
Christmas Delights
Creative Machine Stitching
Crochet for Tots
Crocheted Aran Sweaters
Cutting Corners
Everyday Embellishments
Folk Art Friends
Garden Party
Hocus Pocus!
Just Can't Cut It!
Quilter's Home: Winter, The
Sweet and Simple Baby Quilts
Time to Quilt
Today's Crochet
Traditional Quilts to Paper Piece

APPLIQUÉ
Appliquilt in the Cabin
Artful Album Quilts
Artful Appliqué
Blossoms in Winter
Color-Blend Appliqué
Sunbonnet Sue All through the Year

BABY QUILTS
Easy Paper-Pieced Baby Quilts
Even More Quilts for Baby
More Quilts for Baby
Play Quilts
Quilted Nursery, The
Quilts for Baby

HOLIDAY QUILTS & CRAFTS
Christmas Cats and Dogs
Creepy Crafty Halloween
Handcrafted Christmas, A
Make Room for Christmas Quilts
Welcome to the North Pole

HOME DECORATING
Decorated Kitchen, The
Decorated Porch, The
Dresden Fan
Gracing the Table
Make Room for Quilts
Quilts for Mantels and More
Sweet Dreams

LEARNING TO QUILT
101 Fabulous Rotary-Cut Quilts
Beyond the Blocks
Casual Quilter, The
Feathers That Fly
Joy of Quilting, The
Simple Joys of Quilting, The
Your First Quilt Book (or it should be!)

PAPER PIECING
40 Bright and Bold Paper-Pieced Blocks
50 Fabulous Paper-Pieced Stars
For the Birds
Quilter's Ark, A
Rich Traditions
Split-Diamond Dazzlers

ROTARY CUTTING
365 Quilt Blocks a Year Perpetual Calendar
Around the Block Again
Around the Block with Judy Hopkins
Fat Quarter Quilts
More Fat Quarter Quilts
Stack the Deck!
Triangle Tricks
Triangle-Free Quilts

SCRAP QUILTS
Nickel Quilts
Scrap Frenzy
Scrappy Duos
Spectacular Scraps
Strips and Strings
Successful Scrap Quilts

TOPICS IN QUILTMAKING
American Stenciled Quilts
Americana Quilts
Batik Beauties
Bed and Breakfast Quilts
Fabulous Quilts from Favorite Patterns
Frayed-Edge Fun
Patriotic Little Quilts
Reversible Quilts

CRAFTS
ABCs of Making Teddy Bears, The
Blissful Bath, The
Handcrafted Frames
Handcrafted Garden Accents
Handprint Quilts
Painted Chairs
Painted Whimsies

KNITTING & CROCHET
365 Knitting Stitches a Year Perpetual
   Calendar
Clever Knits
Crochet for Babies and Toddlers
Crocheted Sweaters
Knitted Sweaters for Every Season
Knitted Throws and More
Knitter's Book of Finishing Techniques, The
Knitter's Template, A
More Paintbox Knits
Paintbox Knits
Too Cute! Cotton Knits for Toddlers
Treasury of Rowan Knits, A
Ultimate Knitter's Guide, The

Our books are available at bookstores and your favorite craft, fabric, and yarn retailers. If you don't see the title you're looking for, visit us at **www.martingale-pub.com** or contact us at:

1-800-426-3126
International: 1-425-483-3313

Fax: 1-425-486-7596

Email: info@martingale-pub.com

For more information and a full list of our titles, visit our Web site.